ENNEAGRAM SPIRITUALITY

ENNEAGRAM SPIRITUALITY

From Compulsion to Contemplation

SUZANNE ZUERCHER, O.S.B.

AVE MARIA PRESS
Notre Dame, Indiana 46556

Suzanne Zuercher brings a wealth of experience in spiritual direction and clinical psychology to this, her first book. A member of the Benedictine Sisters of Chicago, she works as a writer and director of workshops and retreats. She regularly conducts enneagram workshops around the world.

A graduate of Loyola University of Chicago, she also earned her master's degree in Clincal Psychology and is a licensed psychologist in Illinois. She has served as a campus minister at Loyola and as co-director of the Institute for Spiritual Leadership. Her articles have appeared in a number of periodicals including *Praying, Human Development* and *Living Prayer.*

© 1992 by Ave Maria Press, Notre Dame, IN 46556

International Standard Book Number: 0-87793-471-1

0-87793-466-5 (pbk.)

Library of Congress Catalog Card Number: 91-76188

Cover and text design by Elizabeth J. French

Printed and bound in the United States of America.

Table of Contents

Introduction _____ 7

1 The First Task of Life _____ 17

2 The Second Task of Life _____ 27

3 Vice and Virtue _____ 33

4 The Story of Mary Magdalene _____ 53

5 The Story of Thomas _____ 59

6 The Story of Peter _____ 65

7 The Meaning of Incarnation _____ 73

8 The Present Moment _____ 95

9 The Contemplative Attitude and Discernment _____ 113

10 The Way to Contemplation _____ 135

11 The Enneagram: A Help to Contemplation _____ 157

Endnotes _____ 167

Introduction

No way of articulating the human situation has proven more helpful in my personal development or in my professional work than has the enneagram. Having been introduced to the initial descriptions nearly twenty years ago, I continue to find them a seemingly endless font of awareness about myself and other people. It is the fruit of these years of reflection that I offer in this book. Its purpose is not to pigeonhole self or others. The intent of any enneagram study ought to be the contemplative pondering and wondering over that creation which is the human person. In this contemplative experience I invite you to join me.

Many people have been exposed to readings or workshops on this system of conceptualizing the human person. If you are one of those, you probably are already concerned, as I am, with considerations beyond these descriptions. It is some of those I discuss in the following pages. If, however, you are unfamiliar with enneagram theory, you will still be assisted to further understandings about yourself and others through these reflections on varying life dynamics and issues.

Several traditions are said to be sources for enneagram theory. The word *enneagram* itself comes from the Greek and refers to a circular figure with nine points on its circumference. In this Sufi philosophy the Divine expresses itself in nine manifestations, which this figure, derived from the decimal system, makes graphic.[1]

A number of authors have treated in detail the history of enneagram theory. I will not repeat their work. Let me say only that all aspects of creation, not only the creation of human beings, have nine different expressions according to the Sufi philosophy. However, it is this enneagram of the human being rather than a philosophical discussion of a theory of creation that is the focus of most contemporary interest in the enneagram.

For myself, a helpful image of enneagram theory applied to those varying kinds of human beings who people the world is that of a prism of light. As one color in a prism gradually shades into the next, so the nine types of personality merge from one to another around this circular figure representing the fullness of human creation. As there is significance and interrelationship among the numbers around the enneagram, so there are nuances of energy, shades, and colors of person, if you will, changing as one space blends to another and that white light which contains all colors is manifest in its varied facets.

The Enneagram and the Human Process

Knowledge about the various ways people view life is enlightening. Realizing the differing ways individuals perceive, process, and respond to their environment not only helps toward self-knowledge, but to understanding ourselves in the context of human relationship. To study the enneagram and to observe the reality of what it describes is to become a more sensitive instrument through whom life can flow for self and others.

As we study the enneagram, we gradually come to see how we frustrate what we most desire for ourselves. We become aware of what clouds our perceptions and blocks our energy. We learn what strikes fear into our hearts and paralyzes them as well as what sends them into automatic, compulsive reaction. We come to know the patterns of personal dynamics and life themes as these recur in experience. Through these awarenesses we can become reconciled with who we are and learn to flow with our life energies. We discover what endowment of ours is a gift for others as well as for us. In other words, we are introduced to our reality more and more. Over time we become better friends of ourselves, discovering where we had made ourselves our own enemy. As more inclusive, more honest, more contemplative awareness of inner and outer reality expands, we grow in consciousness, that experience which makes us human. Denial is less, and the light of contemplative reality shines into our shadow places.

We grow in wisdom as we grow in self-awareness. Life teaches that we will always look at reality from varying vantage points, and the enneagram can help to articulate and expand insights about these. Humility will forever demand that we keep on listening and learning. Humility will also assure and enlarge the perspective that teaches us no single individual has everything to offer. We also find we need patience and humor as we admit our and others' limitations. We grow in forgiveness of ourselves and others, too. The enneagram can move us toward that contemplative life which is the destiny of the human person.

Several books have been written describing each numbered space on the enneagram with distinguishing characteristics of people who flesh out each of the nine. My intention is to move beyond these basic descriptions to a discussion of how the dynamics of each space shape the adult developmental process of people in that stance. *Conversion* or *transformation* or *individuation*[2] are all ways to talk about the task of coming to maturity. Balance and centeredness, both physical and psychic, come about through allowing denied parts of the personality to enter consciousness.

Overview of Differing Dynamics

The early chapters of this book describe what needs to happen for anyone on the adult journey, which is filled with the pain and fear that risk always causes. This process is the universal task, whatever the personality of an individual may be. Even so, each enneagram number faces slightly different issues.[3] There are 2/3/4s, those who respond to life instinctively by doing something about it. In contrast, 5/6/7s instinctively perceive things first, and 8/9/1s have an initial emotional response.[4] The arena of instinctive personal energy—where their life force pulls them—is toward the outer world for 2/3/4s, and they try to

control this world outside them by ordering its activities and
people. Such control gives them a sense of security. On the
other hand, 5/6/7s look for safety by ordering the inner world.
For 8/9/1s the pull of energy from inner to outer and back
again leads them to struggle for power over both.

Dynamics of 2/3/4 Persons

The activity of the 2/3/4s is a byproduct of their anxiety.
They tend to turn other emotions into anxiety because they
are so familiar with it. Fear and anger, for example, may appear
first in their awareness as agitation, a mental script or scenario
of future events or something as simple as a binge of house-
cleaning.

Instinctively social, 2/3/4 people adapt to what they think
the environment and people in it want of them. As a consequence, they may not even notice their own response to things,
let alone their personal needs. They concentrate on connections
among people and assume everyone else does the same. "Who
am I with?" and "How am I doing?" are their spontaneous
questions, both of which focus on life outside themselves.

The present moment is often forgotten. Good or bad old
times color their reminiscence and cause nostalgia for the past.
Plans and tasks and figuring out what to do take them ahead
in time. The present is not a reality; it is only the small crack
that separates past from future, and so it matters little.

The question of adequacy and competence, both measures of
activity, plague 2/3/4s. They look at life in terms of the success
or failure of their achievements or those of others whom they
then assess as better or worse than themselves. It is as though
they carry around with them a measuring stick by which they
compare themselves to everyone else. They either come out
short and feel inadequate, or excel and feel guilty for causing
others to feel inadequate.

They look like emotional people, either cheerful and friendly
or heavy and melancholy. Actually, they have a hard time allowing into their experience and expressing to other people

their emotional life. Emotions are pressed down; this is what "depression" means for them. The real emotional life of 2/3/4s seems to be missing because it is denied. Since it is missing they imitate what others feel and what the environment calls for. The observer experiences the 2/3/4 person as having a brooding, heavy energy or its opposite, overcheerfulness. Neither of these is genuine passionate feeling, something 2/3/4s admire but find hard to "achieve" for themselves. Emotions are not made, they are allowed into experience; all the anxious activity of 2/3/4s crowds them out.

Issues for 5/6/7s

Fear paralyzes the 5/6/7s and leads them to stay in a safe, interior place arranging their gathered perceptions of the world and its people. They search for order inside that will protect them from threat outside and look for where they fit into the scheme of things. They speak of many future possibilities. Often these remain just ideas that 5/6/7s do not turn into concrete plans. Because they tend to wait so long to move out to others, they feel they have been forgotten and overlooked. They often see themselves as of little account. Life and the people in it go on past, leaving them behind, attempting to figure things out.

Because fear paralyzes, actions do not flow naturally as the fruit of their perceptions. Anxiety, which plunges people into action, would force some kind of response were they aware of it in their bodies. Consequently, anxiety hides away and is forgotten for 5/6/7s. Taking in sensory stimuli and ideas, ordering these, and imagining possibilities or consequences flowing from them receive attention and emphasis. Their reality tends to remain an inner one. It does not overflow into decisions which bear fruit in action.

People in the 5/6/7 stance sometimes are called syntony persons. This word refers to an ordering of perceptions received from outside and formulated into some interior system. There is need to find a place for new perceptions, to determine where disparate pieces fit in, whether these ring with or resound with or are in tune with existing perceptions. The issue here is not a moral one as it is for the 8/9/1 person; rather, it is a question of new data being right according to some inner construct or map of reality. The question of searching for this interrelated whole, for syntony, may account for their frequent feelings of being lost, of asking "Where am I?" This is the 5/6/7 question. Syntony leads them to seek where they, as well as their perceptions, belong in the scheme of things.

Syntony includes more than perceptual joining, relating pieces of information, but 5/6/7 people sometimes forget that fact. Their emotional function is what helps them link the world of perception to that of action. The resonance of genuine syntony experience is more than mental resonance. It can be likened to the physical vibrations of a ringing bell. Attention to such vibrations registering in their own bodies can help 5/6/7s discern among possible options where their energy lies. It is affectivity with its consequent felt sense of energy that leads 5/6/7s to that outer world they often find threatening. Genuine emotion can give them the sureness and courage for committed action.

Once they have moved to outer behaviors, 5/6/7 people are less likely to go unnoticed, to be forgotten, to be overlooked. They are recognized by others as well as by themselves when they contribute to their external environment, not only from inside their minds but also where others can observe. Such visibility is a mixed blessing for 5/6/7s. On the one hand they are no longer forgotten; on the other they lose a privacy they treasure and long to preserve.

The 8/9/1 Life Themes

The 8/9/1 people look out at life with another view entirely. Their issues differ because their instinctive response is different. Varying emotions of the 8/9/1s are frequently converted into anger, something at least familiar though not necessarily pleasant. These people instinctively hold their ground rather than adapt to people or circumstances. They have issues around their own personal boundaries. They struggle with where their own boundaries and those of others begin and end. Who they are can be threatened by sweeping waves of emotion that threaten to wash them away. They sometimes feel they are drowning in the emotional intensity of the moment; all they can cope with is this effort to stay above water in the present. Strong affective and bodily responses sometimes make them feel they are bad; surely nobody good would ever get so angry or have such primitive physical reactions.

It is of great importance for 8/9/1 people to feel that they are strong, not only because they overcome themselves but also because they are decisive in relationships with others. They strive to be the powerful ones. To show weakness of any kind would be to let other persons in the contest—and life is a battle to be waged—know where advantage lies. Vulnerable areas might enable others to make inroads and eventually become winners. Emotions of anxiety and fear need to be hidden away from opponents, because these emotions mar the picture of control and strength.

The intense emotional response of 8/9/1s is what frightens them more than anything else. The first person they feel they need to control is the one within. This they try to do by answering their own emotional response with reason and logic. Depending on the individual space among the three, 8/9/1s either consciously curb their emotions by an organized, rational defense or else fail altogether even to be aware that they have strong feelings. The pseudo-logic they use is based on a premise of liking or not liking; around this initial judgment a seemingly objective case in defense of their subjective prejudgment builds up.

Because 8/9/1 persons are so identified with affective response, and affectivity registers in the body, it is common for them to see themselves as less than human. Words they use to describe themselves refer to their animal instincts, of which they are acutely aware. Depraved, sensual, morally rotten, the apple that corrupts and spoils the others in the bushel are typical

accusations they make against themselves before others can do
so. These self-accusations are examples of a kind of control that
looks for power even over their own punishment.

The 8/9/1 persons ask the question "Who am I?" Many
of us ask the same at one or another time, but the felt sense
of it in this space highlights 8/9/1s concern over parameters
and limits. When tides of emotions rise between themselves
and others in relationship, 8/9/1s often find their own personal
boundaries washed away. This experience is the other side of—
and possibly the reason for—strong self-preservation instincts.
Conservation of energy, of time, of involvement are attempts
to keep their individual person from becoming merged with
others. Where self and another begin and end becomes the issue
in their emotion-laden existence, whether they are conscious
or not of the depths of their affectivity.

The Intent of This Book

While these descriptions are brief, they serve to indicate that
not everyone looks at life the same way. We live in different
worlds indeed. It is a wonder we can communicate at all, considering the variety of meanings we put on the very same words
we use so differently as a result of our varieties of life stance
and experience.

There are already a number of books available describing individual enneagram spaces. I think the time has come to move
beyond initial descriptions to more focused studies. That is why
this book emphasizes the process of growing from compulsion
to gift, from dividedness to wholeness, from sinfulness to saintli-
ness. It offers reflections about universal human experience described by the enneagram from a Christian perspective. As you
read about your own basic stance, whether out of knowledge
of enneagram theory, another system, or simply your own life
experience, I hope you will find information that is of personal
value. As you hear about those in other stances, my intention
is to highlight an appreciation of differences in world views
among people. As you learn about who you are and are not,

you may see your own basic dynamics more clearly. You are invited as well to listen in to conversations addressed to other people who know the affliction and joy, as well as the challenge, of their varying and instinctive responses to life.

Of course, I live from only one of the basic instincts myself. In the course of my personal life I believe I have learned things that you may find helpful if you, too, share my world view. If, however, you live in one of the other basic stances, I trust my efforts to describe your dynamics and issues will still be instructive. To that end I have chosen words, images, descriptions, and quotations of people who personally know those experiences.

A Contemplative Approach to the Enneagram

I would like to conclude this introduction with a comment on the subject of moving with or against the enneagram arrows. Such back and forth flow of differing energics links the spaces to one another. There are those who encourage efforts in this regard, who advise people to develop a personal program of meeting the compulsions of their space with the gifts of another space. I do not recommend this approach to personal growth and conversion, nor do I think such an approach assists the process of individuation, of transformation. I hope to develop in these pages a description of Christian maturity that depends on an attitude of contemplation rather than one that emphasizes character-building. This latter approach perpetuates the work of the ego, which I call the first task of life.

Genuine conversion is not a task we can bring about. If we live our lives fully, we will be tested and tempered by such commitment until we are shaped into the person God intends us to be, rather than the one into which we form ourselves. It is for us to come to knowledge of who we are, our light and shadow, our gift and compulsion, our instinct and our excess. Life teaches that information, humbles us, leads us to self-acceptance. From the vantage point of time and wisdom we come to see how we have grown into balance and centeredness because we have been receptive to the human process. Striving to shape ourselves—following or resisting arrows, if you will—prolongs life's first task.

We come to learn in the second part of our lives that life/Life itself makes us into who we were meant to be. Such learning may, indeed, be accompanied by the observation of how arrows have been followed or resisted. But if we set off to make ourselves whole we will, by the very fact of taking control of the process, have ensured its failure. To become a full human being we need to become contemplative, alert, and aware of inner and outer reality as it becomes known to us moment by moment. This book approaches conversion as a contemplative process. In doing so it places conversion on a level deeper than that of ego-development. The following pages will unfold what I mean by the profound reality of coming to that unique word, that self, I am created to be.

CHAPTER 1

The First Task of Life

In the back of my mind hangs a conceptual curtain you need to know about as you read this book. It has to do with the developmental process of a human being. Since everybody's mental backdrop is a little different, I need to tell you about mine. My word choice, allusions, and assumptions in these pages will make no sense without such an initial communication. Bear with me as I try to describe what that backdrop is like. It affects everything else that follows; the story is told against it.

Few of us can even remember a time when adults were thought never to change. Yet that was the perception until developmental psychology looked beyond the child and noticed that adult people, too, were in process. Not only did they need to be so, they couldn't help but be so. Life kept presenting challenges adults continued to meet, and as they did so they were molded by these challenges every bit as much as the child was molded by his or her early experiences of being a human being.

Probably because I live in the 2/3/4 part of the enneagram, I have grouped all of these developmental moments into two main ones, which I call tasks. Granted, I am a behaviorally oriented person, but it is also valid to view life stages as activities to be accomplished. I will examine these two tasks in some detail.

The Paradise Where We Begin

The human story necessarily starts in a Garden of Eden for each of us. Unless it did so we would never have survived past birth. What is this first home we all inhabit for a short time after birth? It is a place of safety and security, of pleasure and peace, a place without worry or anxiety. In this environment a kind and loving Nourisher provides everything we need for life. All of this is so even without our asking for it. We simply find ourselves living in this place, without any reflection on how all of this came about, without question as to its parameters of time or space. It is simply a given and we simply receive. As Sam Keen writes:

> It is my birthright to be loved. The mouth is programmed to expect the breast; the skin claims a natural right to be touched; the heart is quieted only by being in unison with another; the hands reach out to a world presumed to be friendly. We each assume that this place was prepared for us, welcomes us, and rejoices in our becoming. We grow strong in exact proportion to our trust.[1]

This beginning gives us a sense that we are important and valuable to someone. For Adam and Eve in the Garden it was God who provided for them with care. For each of us it is our Providing Mother (or her substitute, perhaps) who conveys a similar message. Adam and Eve, as the story goes, were tempted to move out on their own. Something in their being made them long to be like the God who sustained them. If they were to eat of the Tree of Knowledge they would know both good and evil. What is more, they would become like this God, able to provide for themselves.[2]

We are like Adam and Eve. We also want to become independent. We might say that we want—and also need—to develop our own separate ego, our individual personality. This is a life-giving energy, this urgency to go out on our own. Unless we experience it we remain merely a continuation of our Providing Mother. Now and again articles are written about such people, who spend their entire lives curled in a fetal position in their beds, unable to care for even minimal needs. Of course, this is an extreme situation, but few of us are exempt from moments that hold similar desires and feelings. Most of us know parts of ourselves that now and then wish for such a Paradise, even though we also know life calls us to personal responsibility.

Such separating to become ourselves has another side to it. Why would anyone choose to leave such a place of comfort and security? Why would we ever desire to replace our Nourishing Provider with someone as inexperienced with living as ourselves? The only answer seems to be that we view moving into the direction of our own lives as something we have to do to live. Our question then becomes, what turns our protected and cared-for existence into an undesirable one?[3]

The answer to this question came to Adam and Eve, as it comes to us, shadowed with deception. Yes, we will be like God, knowers of good and evil, people who divide and separate reality for themselves. This is liberating and responsible; it is also deceptive, because God's care for creation is not based on division but on unity and wholeness. God does not make judgments and their consequent boundaries about what exists. Rather, God looks upon everything as good. We are the ones with a fundamental and necessary error, a basic life that ensures the formation of our individual selves. That basic mistake we make is to think we need to be walled off from others in order to survive.

Life on Our Own

Here lies a profound paradox. We do need to create a boundary between ourselves and our Nourishing Provider, or we will never become the persons we were created to be. And yet, to go on in life independently is to experience alienation, loneliness, hostility, and to frustrate our full development. Adam and Eve hid away when the loving God called to them. Eventually they left the Garden to search out another kind of existence.

They had to learn through experiences—struggles and pains, joys and fulfillment, trials and efforts—where life really was for them. We must do the same thing in our individual stories. We learn to hide away from our Nourisher, too. We choose to become our own god, the god who lies to us about what we need. Instead, we must accept the God who authors our existence. We hide away from the one who cares for us by choosing to care for ourselves.

We see how this happens in the Adam and Eve myth. But how does it happen concretely for human beings? Situations vary depending on the circumstances of our history, but the basic plot remains the same for each of us. At some point, probably around the time of the dawning of consciousness, we begin to collect information that gradually adds up to the conclusion we are unloved. We decide that our All Provider does not totally accept who we are, does not allow our being to develop freely.

Instead, we see that he or she places restrictions on what we want for ourselves. The occasion for this awareness might be a casual remark: "Don't bother me now," or "You will sit there until you finish your breakfast," or "That was not a nice thing to do." It might be changes in our family situation, perhaps the addition of a new brother or sister. Feelings of being unloved might result from the illness of a parent or grandparent. Perhaps this sense of abandonment results because of the physical death of father or mother. Parents might divorce. Business travel or wartime service might take a parent away from home for prolonged periods. It might be that something genuinely rejecting occurs, such as physical or mental abuse. But it might be that something is merely perceived to be rejecting. The important thing is that each of us finds—as each of us needs to find—such experiences. Without them we would never begin the movement toward being a separate individual.

Some people spend time searching for that moment when they lost faith in a Nourishing One who would always be there for them. Such a moment may not be as important as is the message we gave ourselves when it happened. One woman I was seeing had searched for months for the cause of her feeling of having to go it alone in life. One day she was looking through old family photographs and found one of herself at age three. In the picture she stood next to her father, untouched and untouching. He held her younger brother on his lap while her mother, sitting beside him, lifted a new baby to the camera. Suddenly she knew how it had happened. Life had told her very early that you have to stand up by yourself.

We might all profit from looking at photos of childhood years. These often catch not only the situations which caused us to separate, but also our response to these situations. When we look at the facial expression or the body posture of the child we once were, we often recognize that child in us still, responding much the same way as we did then.

Our Happy Fault

The Roman Catholic liturgy celebrates this life/death, yes/ no experience at the vigil service for the resurrection of Jesus on Easter. The paradox of it all, the mystery of our human condition, is termed a "happy fault," a necessary sin of Adam and Eve. It is happy and necessary for us, too. Its results lead to our growth and development, even though the price of that growth and development is to cut ourselves off from others, to see them as the enemy, to stop trusting.

This paradox is fault and sin, a short journey from telling ourselves that we are unloved to seeing ourselves as unlovable. Surely, this experience of losing the Provider and Nourisher is to some degree our own fault. Just look at the growing distrust in the eyes of a child as it creates a private life no parent can share.

We are alone and lonely. We need to learn to survive now on our own, to become the god of our own lives, to live outside the Garden. But how can we do this? We are in a world of giants, and it seems more than likely they will trample us to death. How can we make ourselves into people who can hold onto existence? As we answer that question, we begin to create ourselves. We look for and test out those characteristics of mind, feeling, and behavior that will work for us in life. Such decisions and determinations are based on what comes easily and instinctively to us, on what we perceive ourselves as being rewarded for. They are what satisfy our image of ourselves as a survivor.

It is in these earliest instincts, perceptions, and choices that we first see that way of being in life which is our birthright. From our innate enneagram space we censor our environment and its people and events as well as our interior energies. We begin to make ourselves as we choose to be.

Our creation is, of course, limited and finite; we no longer hold in one embrace all that is. We now place judgments on aspects of ourselves. We say, "This is good, this is bad; this will be accepted, this will not." We modify our behaviors into those which the "giant world" will allow, and we suppress those we decide it will not tolerate. Eventually, as with all behaviors we hold inside, unacceptable ones are forgotten and fall out of consciousness and into shadowy darkness.

Those behaviors we find work to our advantage in the giant world we tend to overuse and overemphasize. The result is a distortion of who we really are, a distortion made up of our accenting what we judge as positive and eliminating what we judge as negative. The accented positive becomes our persona or mask, and we wear it for others to see. The eliminated negative is that part of us we hide inside, much of which disappears from our own awareness.

Making Our Caricature

We are no longer, then, the person we were created to be. We are something of a cartoon, an image with exaggerated characteristics based on our judgments of ourselves. We make these judgments out of what we think will help our unlovable selves be loved and accepted and belong. More boundaries exist now: good and bad, inner and outer, conscious and unconscious, light and dark, allowable and not allowable, spiritual and earthly. Our personal god is a god of judgment. We are alone in a world without One Who Cares, both outside ourselves and in our own hearts.

Since this book is directed toward the three basic stances on the enneagram, we will look at some of the ways those in various parts of the circle of creation respond to the life/death, yes/no choice. One man found value in filling another's needs by becoming the significant person in his mother's life. His father had died an early death.

> I was all Mom had to turn to when she felt lonely, and she always seemed to feel lonely. Whenever she would begin to look sad I would start telling funny stories to make her laugh. Sometimes I'd assure her she was the best mother in the world and that everything she did for me was great. Of course this meant I could never let her see my own loneliness and how much I missed Dad myself. I had nowhere to take my own needs, so I buried them and eventually forgot them. I got married when I was thirty. Soon after I began to notice how angry I'd get all the time. I thought my wife was asking for the same thing my mother had. I was tired of giving it.

Another man learned to keep his ideas hidden from other people.

> My memory of childhood is of looking out at the world from behind the big sofa in our front room. Whenever the family gathered together I would run there and hide away, listening to all the others laugh and talk together. I was safe behind there. I could see everybody else but I felt they couldn't see me. My life was my own and nobody could take it away.

The world of spontaneity and feeling is not always a welcome one for the adults we encounter when we are children. In the process of teaching us to adjust to society and its demands, adults sometimes give us messages that we are disapproved of as we are. This girl decided that some aspects of herself were bad and denied their existence within her:

> When I was about four years old, I think it was, I ran into the house where my grandmother was sitting and I started to tell her all about something or other. I don't even remember what it was. I was very animated, probably shouting and jumping around. Grandmother registered disapproval somehow, I remember, and I said to myself "It's bad to get excited. I'll never get excited about anything anymore." From then on I prided myself on being calm, cool, and collected.

Another woman told how she had come to overlook parts of herself in the effort to be thought well of by her family.

> My sister had the good looks. Everybody thought she was beautiful and they sometimes said so in our presence. How could I be important? Well, I was bright and fairly talented. I discovered I had everybody's attention if I said cute things. I pretended I was a television performer and actually worked up a number I did for visitors with songs and dances and stories. I had a feeling of success doing this, and I also noticed myself getting disdainful of pretty girls. After I grew up I would dismiss a potential rival by calling her "beautiful but dumb."

Still another responded this way:

> I tried throwing tantrums for things I wanted. It wasn't long before I discovered there was negative response to this. I was called selfish and neurotic and eventually I began to believe I was. My mother kept threatening to take me to a psychiatrist. When she did, I would get scared and swallow the frustration or anger or whatever it was I was feeling and turn on a happy face. She'd calm down and I decided the only behavior that wouldn't send Mama into anxiety was acting positive and happy. Keep your anger or sadness or fear to yourself. So I did. I now know that when I'm feeling supercheerful I can be pretty sure I'm sitting on "negative" feelings that I've buried.

Whatever it is we do, that choice will fit into how we look at life. For 2/3/4s, pleasant and smooth connections among people will be the intention. The world *is* people for 2/3/4s; all survival decisions are made around that basic perception of life. Instinct prepares for it; censored experiences substantiate it. They let into awareness only what holds up that decision. Out of their innate creation they choose and build the person they judge worthy of love. This is their first task in life, and it must be completed adequately before they turn to the second.

The 5/6/7 people make these same decisions around what will offer safety to them. Arranging the learnings of life into some sort of order and doing that in a private world beyond invasion from the outside is their first task, which brings them at last to a time and situation of readiness. Then they determine to put out for others what they have arrived at in their inner world. Again and again they find that they have waited too long, that nobody is interested in what they have to offer. They discover the moment has passed when all they have thought about and figured out is relevant to other people. Once again they move within to make what they have to say wiser, better, more fitting, in order to earn the love they so much want to have.

For 8/9/1 persons the lesson comes early that people will pay attention to them and they will get what they need by insisting on it in some direct or indirect way. The battle may be won overtly by saying no to a mother who is unable to deal with refusal. Hitting one's head on the floor or fighting with other children may capture concern and attention from parents.

This struggle may be a more passive one: pretending not to hear parental lectures, slowing down precisely because people want them to hurry, refusing to fulfill expectations they know adults in their lives have of them. Messages of power and strength drown out those of weakness and vulnerability. They learn that they are supposed to be strong and take care of their own needs because nobody else in this hostile world will do so. The first task of life involves being in charge of one's individual self and keeping from other people's view that Achilles' heel of vulnerability which would give others the advantage.

The Return to Reality

At this point it might be well to remind ourselves that life is not as neat and orderly as it may seem when I describe it. The task of ego-development, another name for creating myself, is not completed in one day in early adulthood. Neither is it followed the next day by beginning the second task. Nevertheless, it is true that there comes a point when we have a view of ourselves that is positive enough to survive confrontation with more total reality. Then we begin to move into another rhythm of living. We are gradually forced to allow into our awareness some parts of ourselves that we had carefully tucked away out of sight, out of consciousness. Undeniably now, these memories, emotions, behaviors return. They are disconcerting and frightening. They feel like a threat to our very selves, which they are. They begin to destroy that person we have learned to call "self," this "me" we have made from bits and pieces of judgment on our environment and on the persons we see ourselves to be.

The threat of death is at first only hinted at, but it is not long before the terror of complete personal destruction takes over. Overwhelming as this experience may be, it is the beginning of that dying to illusion and delusion that precedes the birth of who we really are. Once again we become acquainted with that person we judged to be bad and unacceptable and whom we hid away in our closet of unconsciousness. We meet parts of ourselves once convicted, sentenced, and crucified. Such re-introduction to our total reality is accompanied by surprise, anguish, and guilt. These responses signal the beginning of life's second task, when we grow to realize the true God is one of love and mercy.

CHAPTER 2

The Second Task of Life

As we enter upon the second task of life, becoming the person we were created to be, we face the consequences of that boundary-making that helped us survive childhood and adolescence and gave us firm predictable parameters for that person we call self. Because of this confidence we learn to face life's challenges and live to tell of them.

It is important to remember that we survived because of numerous lies, as well as truths, that we told ourselves. Having sat in self-judgment we have saved all that seemed good to us and thrown away the rest, imprisoning it in the mist and shadow of forgetfulness. It is the very life experience that encouraged us and testified to our being in charge and in control of our lives that makes us ready now to move beyond the boundaries of self-judgment.

As young adults we begin little by little to realize that we are more than those sure perceptions, acceptable behaviors, and allowable emotions that formed us as we know ourselves. Though we call these new responses bad ones, we cannot deny that they are ours. Yes, this is me, this angry, selfish, enraged, frightened, anxious person. As much as we say, "That's not *me* talking or acting or feeling those feelings," we know it is nobody else. As much as we would like to blame others—and we try to blame others—for what is happening to us, we come to the point, if we are healthy enough, to admit that this is also who we are.

The old boundaries of a kind, adaptable, unselfish, responsive, caring person are gradually widened. We see ourselves more and more as both kind and unkind, adaptable and stubborn, unselfish and self-centered, responsive and insensitive, caring and cold. This awareness comes with no small amount of kicking and screaming on the part of that single-dimensioned, distorted, cartoon-like caricature we have spent our lives creating. At such a time it would be helpful if some image, some analogy, would offer us perspective and allow us to laugh.[1] The pain of watching what feels like our own death would then be less. But it is hard to find humor in so vital a matter.

Trying to Stay in Charge

We are like the Sorcerer's Apprentice in the musical composition of that name.[2] The apprentice thought he knew best how to take care of himself. Eventually, when he could not stop the continuous activity of the broom he had brought to life to do his work, he became desperate. He beat the busy broom into hundreds of splinters, each of which got up and worked again. Then he realized he had only multiplied his problem by trying to end it. He finally accepted defeat and woke up the powerful, napping sorcerer he had tried to imitate. He was ashamed and forced to admit that his scheme was destroying him. He learned he was not his own wise master. He would have to turn to the one who was.

The same thing happens to us. More and more we taste our instincts exaggerated into compulsion. When we try to beat these out of our lives, they only splinter into more and more of the same thing. Our cartoon character takes on monstrous proportions the harder we work to subject it to our control. In the end we, like the Sorcerer's Apprentice, must acknowledge defeat and turn to one wiser than we are. Some people call that wisdom God or the Spirit of God. Others say it is the true self, the whole of me, the one beyond that judge I turn into in order to survive. Still others call it the ground of being, who wakes from the sleep of unconsciousness to be our guide.

The words we use matter very little. This experience beyond the distortions of our self-made ego is one of homecoming, of meeting personal truth and reality. When we touch into our unique word we approach as close to divine experience as human beings can in this life. Julian of Norwich has said that between God and the soul there is no between.[3] Karlfried von Durckheim puts it another way. He describes coming to the ground of one's being as an experience of both the immanence and transcendence of God. Von Durckheim states that the mature person is aware both of the me-ness and more-than-me-ness of the Divine in one single moment.[4]

The human being in touch with his or her center also touches the Life beyond that center, the Being that authors individual being. Perhaps another way to say the same thing is that when we allow our full presence to our full and uncensored reality, our spirit, we also meet that Spirit breathing in all creation.

Of course, this happens in glimpses, in brief moments, over and over again during our lifetime. Maslow talked about "peak experiences," which are probably the same thing.[5] Unannounced and unplanned for, moments of oneness and wholeness and truth come upon us when we least expect them. When such moments become more habitual, when we live more continuously from that center within that asks us for truth rather than perfection, reality rather than deceptions, we are living the second phase of our story.

The Effort of Non-Effort

The second task of life is really not a task at all. It is more the abandoning of the task to create anything out of our lives. If it is action at all, it is the action of letting go, a doing that is even beyond not doing. It exists past any decision not to do. And it comes from the knowledge that we cannot be God in our lives. It is the sense that all of the journeys down all of the avenues of possibility to redeem ourselves are futile. There is nothing we can do that can contribute to our lives. The process of growth is beyond us, not dependent on any efforts we make, least of all on the deceptions we thought essential for survival. At this point we can only surrender to the flow of Life as it is, rather than as we would want to make it be.

What does this surrender based on the necessity to admit our truth feel like? It is the experience of anguish, because anguish is to be aware of, to admit, what we cannot accept and embrace about ourselves. The second part of life involves much anguish. Such pain gradually lessens as we become more humble, simply acknowledging what is so. Over years this admission happens to most of us. There is often a quiet calmness in the eyes of older persons who no longer need to hide their thoughts, feelings, and behaviors from self or others. Such serenity testifies that it is possible to move deeply to a place where we no longer take on the responsibilities of being our own creator. As Jacobi says, "The life and insights we have missed must be made up for item by item, and this ability to live open-eyed with one's own darkness is an achievement that demands courage above everything."[6]

The following are some statements made by people who have moved into life's second task.

> I used to be afraid to be alone. I wasn't sure why, but I said it was because I might get bored with my own company. It's hard even to remember what that felt like. Now I enjoy private time with nobody around. Instead of being afraid of what I might find out about myself when I'm alone, I really believe whatever comes up is good and going to make me better. Besides, I figure everybody else probably already sees it.

> I'm a lot less defensive than I used to be. I can take things in what people say, consider them, and see if they're true of me or not. I used to look like I was doing that, but I was really classifying people as enemies because they brought up unflattering points about me. Now I say "So what? Nobody's perfect." I feel more relaxed and unthreatened than I ever used to.

So what if I'm not the great expert on everything. I think I've understood at last that people would rather know who I am than have me spew off some thought-out analysis of things. That used to be all I thought I had to offer anybody. Now I know it's me they're interested in, at least most of the time. The only way I found that out, though, was by trying out what it was like to give my best friend myself instead of my treatise on some subject.

I spent years trying to figure out how other people were trying to get control over me. One day my counselor asked me to look at that basic premise. Maybe, just maybe, it might be a wrong one. I went home after that session and, for the first time in my life, let my fiance see how scared I was about actually getting married. I found out she was, too, and we had the best talk I'd ever had in my life with anybody. Just the first of many, I'm happy to say.

Becoming Our Own Friend

In *The Interior Castle* Teresa of Avila speaks of the importance of being able to draw near to one's self on the spiritual path. Without such approach to the self there can be no growth. She says that the sinner is one who does not love self enough.[7] What we learn in this second part of life is that what makes us sinners is not so much the thing we judge to be wrong or bad, but our misconception about what life is meant to be. We learn that we are creaturely and therefore imperfect. We will never be all-knowing, all-wise, all-beneficent, no matter how hard and long we struggle to be. We are not God.

Eventually we come to appreciate how good it is that we are not, judgmental and self-punitive as we tend to be. In the process of finding out we are only creatures, we also find out that there is a Divine Nurturer who knows—who has always known—everything about us, including those parts we could never look at. We find a Creator who is comfortable with the reality of creation, not one who is dissatisfied or demands the impossible. And what is impossible is our perfection.

How easy all of this sounds. In reality, this process is the greatest of life's sufferings. Traveling deeper each day and year into that dark valley feels like death—and is so to our self-deceptions—and takes more courage than any other of life's challenges. We would never be able to continue on this path were it not for an evergrowing sense of rightness and fittingness about this process. A peaceful sureness lies beneath the terror and turmoil our struggling, created self experiences near the surface.

A Continuing Journey

This second task of life is never over. We continue to learn and relearn the lesson of life. However, as our compulsions become ever harder to deny, most of us grow more comfortable with them. In desperation we gradually learn to make peace with what we cannot get rid of. We become more and more like the God who knows and receives our entire person. A friendliness toward once unwelcome, alien aspects of ourselves enables us to be gradually more open toward others as well. No longer are our problems blamed on others' limitations and evil because we are unable to admit them as parts of us. We realize now that we are not victims of other people who are our enemies, but that our enemy is within. We are victims, indeed, but victims of our own inner victimizer. Our sin is nonacceptance of ourselves. St. Teresa knew what she was talking about.

Vice and Virtue

Enneagram theory often uses the words *vice* and *virtue* to describe those instincts which are compulsive and those which constitute the giftedness of a certain space. These two words sound like opposites. I propose, however, that they are part of a continuum. The very instinct we accentuate to the point of compulsion in ourselves is also the source of our greatest contribution to self and others, the contribution which is ours to creation.

Each of us manifests divinity. Since we are so limited as creatures, we can only hope to witness to divine presence in some small way out of who we imperfectly are. Some profound, if distorted, wisdom led us to choose certain aspects of ourselves to develop. This choice took place at that fundamental experience of rejection and alienation which began the task of self-creation I have termed ego-development.

It might be well to remind ourselves that we look out at life from different places depending on our enneagram stance. What we judge to be important for life, our values, what we tend to overlook in ourselves and the world around us depend on our innate endowment. In the first task of life we concentrate on what is apparent to us in our personalities. This obvious part becomes—partly because it is so instinctive—what we hear others rewarding us for. After all, we do have facility in some areas. To become persons who can survive in the world, we need to perceive as being told, and also tell ourselves, that this facility we have is the best one. And so the making of our cartoon character begins. We are bent on self-creation and start to reinforce these instincts into compulsions.

The Basic Instincts

What does this process look like for people around the enneagram circle? What is that instinct that we know so well, even at the early time of separation from the Nourishing Mother? Granted, no one sits down and decides consciously how to become a survivor. This just seems to happen. The happening is, however, based on a store of information we have within and upon which life urges us to draw. Another way to look at what occurs is to ask ourselves how in any given moment we respond to life, the people in it, and ourselves before we are aware. This question will surface the innately instinctive in our personalities.

For 2/3/4s the answer to such an inquiry is that they meet everything outside as well as inside from their activity function. To put it another way, they are doers. They "do" life. Life is a task, first of all, and they work at accomplishing it. They begin to do before any conscious choice is made, working to ensure an environment in which they can remain connected to others.

The 5/6/7 persons instinctively perceive. For them life is a problem they need to address, to work out, to make sense of. They find themselves taking in data of all kinds from the world around them and ordering it inside. Before they are even conscious of what is going on they observe reality, looking for ways to make sense of the discrete and disparate information coming to them from many sources. If they can succeed in finding that which will make everything fall into place, they feel they will be wise and, consequently, safe.

Life as a battle, or at least a struggle, leads 8/9/1s to be on guard and ready, covering their own vulnerable areas while they sniff out those of their opponents. They instinctively ask where power lies and test out the answer. If this life is warfare, then they must win. To yield means at least imprisonment, if not death. In fact, to have personal freedom taken away is much like dying. Before there is any consciousness, these people are poised for struggle and determined to win in order to survive.

Persons in all enneagram stances initially assume that there is no other kind of response than their own. Early on in life they think all people approach reality in much the same way they do. Later on they are amazed to discover that other people are different. One of the most valuable learnings about the enneagram is the realization that, no matter how enlightened people become, they will always retain an instinctive world view, an outlook on life, characteristic of their basic stance.

People in the 2/3/4 stance work to assure an environment in which they remain connected to other people, while 5/6/7s try to order their inner world of perceptions and 8/9/1s struggle to gain or retain power over themselves and others. There is nothing deliberate in this adapting or ordering or looking for power. That is the meaning of instinct; it is automatic.

Even while we come to acknowledge that others are different from ourselves, at first this is unimagined and unimaginable. Although later in life we realize that others' spontaneous reactions differ from our own, we still can never know these reactions experientially. That, too, is what it means to have our innate instinct.

The Journey Symbolized in the Body[1]

One way to make more concrete some of what I am saying is to look at those portions of the body that hold blocked energy and interrupt the flow of life. For 2/3/4s this area is the skeleton of the torso. The bones of chest and shoulders, the rib cage, the backbone and pelvis serve as defense for the softer, more pliable, even pulsating inner organs. This skeleton covers the body's interior activity like armor. It also holds the body upright and prepared to keep going. Problems that deeply affect the well-being of the body are hidden beneath this hard covering and are disguised by it. Efforts for 2/3/4s center on "not falling apart" and "keeping moving." Competence and capability are of primary importance as are accomplishment and success.

The issue that such emphasis raises is one of sensitivity to the subtle changes and inner experiences of the self. The issue is knowing their own needs and responses, so hidden are they beneath a hard sort of efficiency and productivity. Instead, it is the outer world that draws attention. Clues about personal experience, well-being or dis-ease, are sought from the environment and people in it. Persons in this stance can only know what is well and not well with them from outer data. Erect, ever-driving, and ever-striving bone structure keeps them far from experiential knowledge of how life affects them inside.

What they do not know, their emotional response to the world they live in, becomes part of that hidden and ultimately forgotten shadow. This response is a felt sense that does not seem important in their view of life. Instead, it is the world of activity, effort, and functioning that is real—or at least conscious. Out of that conviction they set about making a life for themselves, a life of accomplishment and product. The kinds of functioning that are important will differ at each of the enneagram points in the basic stance. Some people see acts of service as primary.

> I was always doing something for somebody. It was a driven
> sort of thing. I don't think I ever asked anybody I was helping
> whether they wanted me to or not. I just did it. Anything
> at all just to make me feel good about myself.

For others it is success in some form: good grades, impressive job descriptions, associating with people of status and gaining status oneself, attaining the pinnacle of the corporate ladder, knowing the best people, having the most desirable relationships.

> When my son told me he wanted to be a carpenter I couldn't
> believe it. I told him our whole family had been professional
> people for generations. He said he didn't care about them,

> but he knew what he wanted for himself. I still find it embar-
> rassing to tell people what he does. I've even caught myself
> telling others that he's a furniture designer. What's the big
> deal for me? I don't know, but obviously there is one.

For still others, value comes from authoring something
unique and different, surrounding oneself with what one judges
to be a refined, beautiful, enhanced environment or relationship.

> When my brother was a kid he always wanted the best edi-
> tion of any children's book. He said it was the beginning
> of his private collection. He's still kind of a snob. If it isn't
> a leatherbound volume it's his Mercedes, and not for the
> engine, but the class.

For the 5/6/7s it is the perceptual instinct centered in the
head, and especially the eyes, that is instinctive. Therefore, in
the first task of life, perception is exaggerated. This place where
the brain is located stands for the interior world of ideas and
perceptions and their relationships. Reality enters through the
doorway of the eyes and is put together in the head, or so we
speak of what happens. Every moment brings something new
to internalize. Therefore the task of fitting new data with what
is already there never ends. Because they are instinctively afraid
of the outer world and uncomfortable functioning in it, 5/6/7s
choose to remain inside and continue their inner work. Fear
freezes body response in this space. Such paralysis of the body
reduces activity to that of gathering information.

The emotion that 5/6/7s early in life learn to bury into unconsciousness is anxiety. Of its nature anxiety agitates the body
and urges one to action. When one perceives the world and
those in it as threatening, one needs to have a disposition that
encourages and continues withdrawal to a safe place. For 5/6/7s
that safe place is their inner world, where they fit new stimuli
into proper association with what is already there. The upset
and chaos that moving out might cause is avoided. The body

does not experience impulses to action triggered by anxiety, and so fear protects continued perception.

Response to this dynamic differs in the three numbers of this gesture. Some 5/6/7s pull within and remain there. Others move back and forth, alternately withdrawing and rushing out again. Still others attempt behaviors that are withdrawing and disengaged while they appear to be interacting with people.

The image of a city subway station might help here. Some people, as a train screams in and grinds to a stop, tossing dirt and papers around and causing people to crush toward train doors, pull away against a wall in an effort to protect themselves. Others begin with this same response, but realizing they must get on the train or else fail to continue their journey, lunge forward just in time to catch the train. Some of these people delay so long that by the time they consider themselves ready to move they have only a daring and reckless option available to them: they must grab onto the final, moving car as it disappears into the subway tunnel. Still others want to withdraw, but they know how important it is to keep moving out despite fears. They push down initial inner terror and plow into the milling crowd, assuring themselves a place on the subway train.

While this is merely an analogy, it does indicate the variations in response throughout the 5/6/7 space. One woman describes her dynamics when she attends small group meetings.

> I'm always well-prepared when I get there. In fact, I think I'm better prepared than most. But I usually don't say anything. By the time I know what it is I want to say and have put it together in my mind, somebody else has already articulated something similar. So I keep quiet. Why say substantially the same thing over again? But usually at the end of the meeting someone will ask me what I think and so I tell them. You wouldn't believe how angry some people get because they think I've deliberately withheld an insight. I haven't. I just figured it must be obvious to everybody else because it was to me.

Another person, a young man moving into an intimate relationship, addresses shifting back and forth from fear to outrage and paralysis to action.

> I certainly care for my friend and want her near me. So I invite her in, invite her to come closer. When she does come, I get scared. I feel invaded, crowded. I realize what I've done; I've given away my protection and my privacy. So I run and hide again and then my friend tells me she feels like I just pulled up the bridge across the moat from my side. But there's nothing else I can do at that moment. Maybe later on I can go back and try again. But right then I just run.

The fear of losing one's private life and ordered perceptual world is not always revealed exteriorly, except through the eyes. While the body clues may be minimal for 5/6/7s, one place where their inner reality is expressed is through what writers have long called the mirrors of the soul.

> I was chatting away with Sarah and I thought I was pretty relaxed considering I didn't know her very well as yet. Then she turned to me and said "What's wrong with you? You look absolutely terrified. I'm not going to bite you." I had no idea how she knew I was scared. In fact, I hadn't known how very frightened I was until she put her finger on it. She said my eyes gave me away.

People in the 8/9/1 stance have their instinctual center beneath the skeleton of the torso. Here are the softer, more flexible organs: stomach, bowels, liver, kidneys, but especially the heart. The rhythm of life is felt strongly pulsating in this area. The heart is a vital organ; it is also vulnerable to attack. Response from the heart can be seen and heard as it reacts against or accepts environmental stimuli. It will accelerate its beat or slow down depending on these stimuli, and this response resonates through the body. Life itself depends on the heart. No wonder it symbolizes the totality of persons as well as their emotional life.

The 8/9/1 people instinctively respond to life all of a piece, as it were. It is not instinctive for them, as it is for 2/3/4s, to stand next to aspects of themselves and relate to them. They do not so much "have" a body as they "are" a body; their bodies are themselves. Their ideas and opinions and prejudices are also themselves. So, too, are their emotions. They do not "have" anger; instead, they are blinding rage. They do not have fear or anxiety; they become a frozen mass or a twanging nerve end. No wonder 8/9/1s want to protect whatever is going on with them. Someone could take advantage of their "being blown away" because they lose awareness until the intensity of the moment has passed.

Because they respond so deeply and totally to what is happening in the present, 8/9/1s do all they can to remain in control of themselves. They are also alert to vulnerable spots in others. They need to look powerful, so they respond with powerful expressions of that strength or else with a calm and control that covers their vulnerability. No wonder, also, that they watch for opportunities to take advantage of other people. The best defense is a good offense, and knowledge of the opponent's weaknesses allows for a better struggle or battle and, ultimately, better warfare.

Wars for 8/9/1s are fought to determine who will have control over outer territories or inner space and personal freedom; territory, whether inner or outer, is something of which 8/9/1s are very aware. They do not want to lose theirs or have it invaded. Instinctively they protect their own boundaries from threat; they are also alert for invasion of other people's boundaries. When an invader threatens someone less powerful, they can be strong protectors of the disadvantaged.

Overwhelmed by wave after wave of emotional response and by that basic feeling of like or dislike, attraction or repulsion, 8/9/1s easily "lose their heads." The perceptual function which observes and orders stimuli is gone. Deep in the shadow falls objective appraisal of reality, and life is lived as the heart dictates. Sometimes there are efforts to become rational, but dry, lifeless reason is a meager substitute for genuine perception, which offers perspective, and interrelates and sets priorities. Cold and logical though they appear, the attempts of 8/9/1s to counter instinctive feeling responses are subjectively based. They build a supposedly objective case around their affective conclusions. What they like they uphold; what they do not like they argue against.

A young man describes his approach as a college debater:

> First I build up my case. I need to sound very cool, even when I'm steaming underneath. You can't let yourself get carried away. I'm very alert for flaws in my opponents' arguments, and even more, in themselves. It doesn't take me long before I know how and how not to catch them and make them slip. After a tournament—I usually win in tournaments—I really feel great. Nothing can stop me.

Sensitivity to boundaries, one's own as well as those of others, can make a champion out of the 8/9/1 person:

> I was the oldest in my family and I took my job of big sister seriously. I never hovered over the littler ones, but I watched out to make sure nobody took advantage of them. I remember teaching my little brother how to fight for himself. I don't think he ever did fight, though. It didn't seem to be his thing to do. I guess people are just different.

Some people in this space find it hard to admit the strong affective responses which lead to perceptual blackouts. A woman describes how she became aware of her anger at her unfaithful husband only after having the following dream:

> I was riding on what seemed to be a huge dragon. It had fire coming out of its eyes and ears and nostrils and it was making deep, growling sounds. My husband was eating a picnic lunch on the beach with his secretary and I stampeded the place and trampled all the food. Then the dragon crushed Joe's head under one foot. I woke up shouting "Good, good, good." My husband was sleeping beside me and he asked me what was wrong. I couldn't say anything, so I just apologized

for waking him up and gave him a kiss. He turned over and
went back to sleep. But I didn't.

Places of Instinctive Energy

The criterion for evaluating what is important does not come
from inside for 2/3/4 people. They are separated from the inner
world by the skeletal wall, which holds them up even as it
holds them off from their vital interior responses. This armor
symbolizes the hard barrier they set up early in life to hide from
themselves those emotions that might cripple their competence.
They look to the outer world and to those who live there for
their values and for proof they are living up to them. What
people say, what earns approval and reward, what pleases those
around them, what prevents conflict and separation, dictate how
2/3/4s live life and make choices.

Their constant concern is that others find them acceptable.
Their vision is always outside and ahead, where what they are
doing now will either be assessed favorably or unfavorably at
some future time. They cannot be said to be attentive to the full
reality of any given moment. They do not truly "see" others in
their world. They aim at goals and accomplishments ahead of
them in time; even their physical gaze is focused there. Because
they are taken up with something future, they are concerned
with what is nonexistent. They measure their activity, what
they judge to be most valuable, not by reality but by something
imagined.

The criterion for what matters comes from inside for 5/6/7s.
Their eyes bring in what is important to their inner world,
where they can be involved with fitting new information into
their established order or system. Whether what comes from
outside fits or not is what matters to them. It is important to
be right, to know what things mean so they can feel in control of the inner world where they spend most of their time.
They look for others who view things as they do. This gathering of supportive evidence from others whom they consider
knowledgeable confirms their own insights.

Because they are concerned with data, 5/6/7s can be quite literal. They take at face value what someone says. They are attentive to words, and playing with them in word games and puns is an enjoyable activity for many in this stance. It is difficult for 5/6/7s to accept what others say when it does not resonate with their own perceptions. 5/6/7 people depend on what they see, and find it important to validate personally what they have been told about but have not observed firsthand. They sometimes do not truly "hear" other people in the nuances of their emotions or the recounting of their personal histories. They can become disengaged from the reality of the other and treat that other with cold objectivity, examining personal revelations as purely factual data.

For 8/9/1s, their instinctive judgment of like or dislike forms the basis for every response that follows. When they are in compulsion, whether a cause is to be espoused, a person accepted, or an idea embraced depends on their attraction or repulsion to it rather than on the reality of that cause, person, or idea. It is not easy for 8/9/1s to realize and accept that despite their instinct to measure everything and everyone fairly, they are often motivated by prejudice that prevents access to the truth. They tend to fixate on their judgment of things and people, mistaking that judgment for what is so. Unlike the 5/6/7s, who keep looking for information to substantiate their views, 8/9/1s reinforce their initial judgment with arguments supporting it.

In their compulsive state, 8/9/1s neither see nor hear what is going on around them. Instead, they build up their case and their plan of action around a preconceived notion that forms the basis for all that follows. Those whom they assess as right, and values and concepts they assess as good, become important. There is a heavy moral sense both in themselves and in what they choose to invest or from which they withhold their energy. They see themselves as either upholding or not upholding the morally good. In the latter case, they perceive themselves as cowardly or lazy or stubborn, all of which are judgments that they are bad.

The Role of Anxiety

Anxiety is the particular province of 2/3/4s. Anxiety plunges them into action. It feels like restlessness, like the impetus to do. Therefore, it is a natural accompaniment for those who are instinctive doers. What are they anxious about? All that they are working toward, making plans for, wanting to be accomplished. They write scripts that they can then apply to imagined future situations. These scenarios give them a semblance of being in control. If they can cover in fantasy all the possible future events, they feel "on top of" their lives and in charge of their existence. They can be the all-powerful gods in their own behalf.

They view themselves as responsible for the world outside them and the functioning of people and situations in it. Because of this attitude, 2/3/4s spend much energy in their instinctive state maintaining the bonds of this outer world. To that end they sacrifice all else, even deceiving others and lying to them if necessary.

The Role of Fear

5/6/7s instinctively become frozen with fear. By its nature fear paralyzes; it prevents them from doing anything but collecting more and more information upon which to base a wise and sure judgment. Given enough time, perhaps they will find the response that makes everything fit into an ordered whole, or so they think. There is some key, they are certain, that answers all questions of meaning and rightness in the universe. To that end they search; to that end they gather information. But none offers that final satisfaction; none puts them "on top of" their lives, safe in a world of ordered system.

In their compulsive state 5/6/7 people find it impossible to come to the feeling that precedes genuine decision-making, the sense that can capture them and move them into action. As long as they continue at the merely perceptual level, they can continue gathering information and postponing decisions. The benefit of this dynamic is that it prolongs the safe atmosphere of their inner world. Having instinctively moved within and buried the anxiety that propels to action, they restrict their doing to formulating possibilities and options. In this way they need not make their inner experience concrete outside themselves.

The Role of Anger

For 8/9/1 people, it is anger which is the most familiar—though not necessarily pleasant—emotion. Other feelings become translated into anger, which then produces a sense of strength and power. Rather than admit fear, 8/9/1s under pressure retain their invulnerable and offensive position, forgetting or pushing down gentler feelings that might leave them undefended. In this way they can appear invincible to themselves and others. If they are angry at their sorrow or fear, they can stay in charge of their reactions and have the sense that they are "on top of" their reality. Inwardly, this dynamic makes them feel stronger than the vulnerable emotions of sorrow, anxiety, and fear, which otherwise might wash them away; outwardly, they feel ready to cover those areas where another might attack them.

For some 8/9/1s the most effective way to deal with emotion is to put it down entirely. Emotions of all kinds must submit to the invincible "I." The result is a flat, lethargic boredom with one's own life and a need to look for stimulus, for meaning, for engagement outside the self. 8/9/1s who either deny or rein in their emotions lose a sense of commitment. They become heady and logical or overbearing and tough instead of passionate and dedicated. They substitute involvement in causes for personal engagement. When this happens they become aware at some level that they have lost the integrity to live from both weakness and strength. Such lack of honesty is not only cowardly, it is immoral in their eyes.

The Question of Lying

Some people say 2/3/4s are liars, but I do not think they lie any more than people in other spaces. A harmonious and connected environment is the top priority for 2/3/4s. To that end they sacrifice everything, including reality itself.

In the 8/9/1 space the most important value is integrity. For 8/9/1s it is essential to have a congruence, a resonance, between inner experience and the outer expression of that experience, to have a yes that is truly yes and a no that is genuinely no, as scripture says (Mt 5:37). To withhold what they are experiencing is seen as deception.

5/6/7s use the word *truth* to describe what they believe is of the essence. For them, truth is a rightness, a fittingness, that makes reality real. For something to be true, it needs to be in proper relationship to everything else; it needs to belong in its appropriate position in the scheme of things.

Because of these differing ways of looking at reality, persons in the 5/6/7 and 8/9/1 spaces need to lie through illusion and delusion, need to deceive themselves about what is real, shaping it into an appearance of truth. 2/3/4s simply name a value above authenticity: the value of smooth relating.

The Question of Sensitivity

Perhaps it would be most accurate to say that all people under the demand of their compulsions are insensitive. The particular kind of insensitivity in the 2/3/4 spaces is invasion of others' lives and manipulation of the environment and people in it. This outer world is the only place where any semblance of control can be maintained. The hidden interior of deeply experienced emotion has long ago been pushed from awareness, largely because it interferes with efficient functioning. In that world of inner affections 2/3/4s feel like strangers.

For 5/6/7s the inner world they inhabit provides refuge. Their insensitivity is around maintaining such an environment for themselves. They become aloof and disengaged when this world is threatened and withdraw to their perceptual mode. People outside can feel cut off from affective encounter with them. The experience others have when 5/6/7s disengage in this way is of becoming objects for study rather than persons for encounter.

In their efforts to remain strong and invulnerable 8/9/1s have an insensitivity that feels harsh and brusque. When their more gentle emotions are evoked in relationship and they become frightened about losing control of the situation, they take on a tough, protective exterior. People who relate to them in such circumstances feel scolded or punished, held off or resisted.

Where, then, can people find a sense of control that perpetuates the illusion of being divine? The 2/3/4 intrusion, clinging, and manipulation of the outer environment clashes with the cold and distant aloofness of 5/6/7s and the harsh and aggressive resistance of 8/9/1s. We are all little gods colliding on the battlefield of the present moment. We have our particular self-investment and self-interest expressed in our particular type of compulsive tendency.

Coming to a Place of No Exit

Given all of this, it might seem that the only way to human reconciliation and peace is to attack these instincts grown to the monstrous proportions of compulsion. For all of us it would seem necessary to eliminate those traits—or at least the exaggeration of those traits—that cause conflict, pain, and unrest for others as well as for ourselves. But this is not the case, even though such a solution involves just what we think, early on, that life is all about: effort and accomplishment.

Our full-blown compulsions are the fruit of the efforts to build our ego, which is our initial task in life. Later we are asked to allow into consciousness all of those aspects we had to deny to become the cartoon character we came to call ourselves. What we must *not* do if we are to arrive at the fullness of the word God created us to be, is continue to exaggerate effort. We must not even "give up effort," which is also an activity. Then, what are we to do? Nothing? And yet, to do nothing is to *do* no thing, which is again doing something.

Yet all of us find ourselves falling to a place of inner truth, of honest humility. We cannot bring about our transformation, least of all when we try to do so by our own powers. Such trying merely grinds more deeply the groove of compulsion. Perhaps we must come to—in contrast to "go to," which puts us in charge—recognition of our constant, unceasing question: What can I do to become whole? Perhaps what we most need is a simple awareness of that early consuming compulsion to create someone who will belong and be loved.

Surely there is more that we can "do" than merely to notice our reality, to see what happens again and again in our lives. How will change ever come about without some efforts toward it? Yet the very efforts perpetuate our slavery. We remain unfree and compulsive, unchanged from the point of view of conversion. If our lives are to turn around, we need simply to acknowledge and admit our reality as it becomes known to us.[2] And this we cannot accomplish for ourselves. Eventually, after exhausting attempts to prove otherwise, we are surprised by the realization that we are not God. Such acknowledgment is given to us; it cannot be earned, planned for, worked toward.

From Control to Contemplation

When awareness of this truth—which is the essence of contemplation—becomes more and more part of who we are, change happens. In the second task of our lives we relax into the knowledge that change happens, reality shapes us, there is nothing we can do to save ourselves. No matter what our enneagram stance, we all come with simple clarity to know that precisely what we accomplish best is our own enslavement.

Once we have realized our compulsive self-victimization, what then? Do we become totally inert? What happens to us when we become aware of how every effort of ours deepens the groove of our compulsive living? What happens as we grow into the true selves we were meant to be? We are not essentially evil; we do not need to lose our very being.

Here we have the wonder of redemption. We are not delivered from our native endowment. It is that very distinguishing characteristic that becomes our contribution to creation. People who are 2/3/4s will always function easily in the outer world, see genuine needs, get things done, accomplish goals, be competent and capable and efficient. Those who are 5/6/7s will retain the ability to shape the inner world into order and meaning, to form a seemingly chaotic universe into a perceptual whole, to relate the new to what already exists. Those in the 8/9/1 stance will continue to see where power resides, to use that power to work for justice, to enable others to empower themselves.[3]

The world needs all of us, but only when we are no longer deluded into thinking that the caricature we have made of ourselves is all we are or need to be or can be. Once this instinct, which we exaggerated into compulsion, assumes proper proportion in our lives it becomes a natural and free response. We no longer need to force ourselves to be doers alone if we are 2/3/4s. We can let go of the need to cover our pliable, warm, changing, limited interiors. Our armor can be removed and we can relax. We can allow other aspects of ourselves to emerge, some of which may not contribute to a smooth, acceptable, and efficient environment. But we will always be most at home in the world of action and task. We will accomplish what needs accomplishing, though more and more gently as life goes on.

If we are 5/6/7s, we no longer need to hide away in the safe world of perception. We can venture forth, little by little, letting emotional engagement as it registers in our bodies energize us and take us beyond fear and withdrawal. We can share our selves with other people, giving them our feelings and our deeds as well as our perceptions. We can risk letting others know that we do not see how everything fits together, that we are not always resonant with other people and their ideas. But we will always be most at home in that inner world, offering insights into life and its significance, more and more gently as life goes on.

If we are 8/9/1s, we become freer to acknowledge and flow with the passionate emotions of our inner and outer living. We hold our world as a whole, no longer seeing power and weakness as contradictory, no longer dividing life into warring opposites. We can risk being vulnerable, losing with individuals we love and in causes to which we are dedicated. We accept powerlessness and limitation. Inwardly, our ability to perceive in analogy and to shape life through image and symbol offers personal perspective; outwardly, our removal of boundaries between ourselves and others inspires efforts toward unity and peace in our world, more and more gently as life goes on.

If we are 2/3/4s, our acknowledgment of who we are will be so authentic that we will no longer need to turn activity inward and call it self-analysis. We will no longer need to tell ourselves that doing is our only contribution and our only way to survive in a hostile world. Because we will drive ourselves less, others will experience themselves as less driven and manipulated by us.

If we are 5/6/7s, we will become so truthful that we will no longer see the outer world as a place of threat. We will no longer need to protect our inner world from invasion of hostile forces that would ridicule or upset the meanings we have worked so hard to order. Our suspicion of others will be unmasked as fear of chaos, and we will reveal ourselves in a more open way to a world we will now accept as friendly.

If we are 8/9/1s, we will become so full of integrity that we will let ourselves see our own interior reality with its strength and weakness and allow others to know this same strength and weakness. We will no longer need to face our hostile self and a hostile world with an image of invincibility. Consequently, because we are both strong and weak, we will be able to let go and be shaped by our inner and outer experience.

Living With Our Reality

We will not actively have cut out the condemned aspects of who we saw we were. We will have grown into a perspective about ourselves that allows us to see how absurd we have been and to laugh at that absurdity. If we are 2/3/4s, we will be doers who neither glamorize doing nor work at stamping it out. If we are 5/6/7s, we will be perceivers who acknowledge who we are, and who realize that we will always find it difficult to move into the world and turn our perceptions into desired actions. If we are 8/9/1s, we will come to realize that all of our responses will be colored with emotion, and that such is and always will be our reality. We will be reconciled more and more with who we simply are. We will judge and blame ourselves less and less. We will pity the paradoxical struggle of our paradoxical selves more and more.

Gradually that view of ourselves will open us to a clearer view of others. We will begin to "see" those around us here and now if we are 2/3/4s. We will "hear" others if we are 5/6/7s. We will waken to both "see" and "hear" if we are 8/9/1s. And other people who struggle and judge and blame themselves as they try to survive in life will be viewed more tenderly—and humorously, too. We, who now know what monsters and kind givers we can be and are able to live in peace with that knowledge, will also live more and more in peace with others. They also have struggles, distinct from, yet parallel to, our own.

We know we have a gift of doing or perceiving or feeling to offer the world; we know how we can frustrate that gift, and do frustrate it, by constant attempts to "make" ourselves. Just knowing all of this helps. It turns what once was a blind, compulsive lifestyle into a more humble, contemplative one. It does so not by denying our basic instinct, but by realizing it. We see how our virtue becomes our vice and our vice our virtue, and how life is a constant tossing of the coin of instinct. Sometimes it comes up on one side and sometimes on the other.

As we yield to the continual process of existence—which is yielding to the Creator—we find Life happening within us and around us. And more and more in this second rhythm of our existence we marvel at the mystery.

CHAPTER 4

The Story of Mary Magdalene

Gospel stories often reveal the enneagram spaces of people in them, because human nature remains basically the same through every age. Most of those authors from former centuries never heard the word *enneagram*, but it is not surprising to find them describing three kinds of responses to life. The Johannine community, which authored the gospel we attribute to John, tells of Jesus' appearance to three persons after his resurrection from the tomb.[1] In each story we observe characteristic behavior of the people involved and listen to Jesus' response to that behavior. We also learn what mission was assigned to each according to his or her personality with both its virtue and its vice. Jesus reminds all three of the compulsions characteristic of their spaces. He also tells them how the very traits that lead to compulsions can be transformed and used in the service of God's kingdom.

For information about the 2/3/4 compulsion and trap, as well as that gift which is theirs to give, we will reflect in this chapter on Magdalene's story. If we are 2/3/4s we have much to learn about ourselves, our mission in life, and our relationship with Jesus that her story can make clear.

A Story of Anxiety

Magdalene's story within the context of Jesus' gospel story began early on the first day of the week, so early that the sun had not even risen.[2] We need to recall that Jesus' body had been quickly taken down from the cross and placed in the tomb with–

out proper anointing and preparation for burial. The sabbath sundown prevented those loving services, but Magdalene had not forgotten them. She waited the prescribed time until she was free by law to leave home and conclude the burial washing and anointing.

We can only imagine what the preceding day had been like for Magdalene. She had lost her most intimate friend, the man who had brought meaning to her life and whom she loved as she had never loved anyone else. She had adapted to others' desires in many ways throughout her lifetime, but Jesus had offered her companionship that contributed to a self-respect and self-valuing she had never known before. Now he was dead and she was alone, confused, and waiting for some indication of what such love and loss might mean for her future.

How did she express this feeling of lonely emptiness? Magdalene's response was characteristic, as everyone's is in crisis. She began to do what she felt she must do as soon as Jewish law would allow it. Apparently she was concerned about what would happen were she to violate this greatest sabbath of the year, and this concern may well have taken the form of what people would think of her were she to do so.

For whatever reason, she did observe the law, refraining from that activity which alone would express her love. As soon as custom allowed her to do so she set out for the grave, dealing with her sorrow by planning acts of care and service to Jesus. She intended to spend this quiet time tending to his remains while she mourned the loss of the life that had so filled her own with meaning.

Doing Instead of Feeling

How characteristically 2/3/4! Feelings, profound though they be, rarely leave people in this stance motionless. That intense anxiety into which they translate other feelings keeps them ever on the move. There is no better way, they think, to show love than by care, attention, and service. This is true especially when they suspect that the emotional richness observed in other people is somehow not theirs to give. When they have recognized and named what they are feeling, there remains only the decision as to what to do about it.

People in the 2/3/4 space are observers of their emotional life rather than participants. They do have feelings; these feelings are someplace within them as part of who they are. Feelings can be looked at and assessed. But rarely are 2/3/4s "taken" by them, bathed in them, as one might be who stood covered and enveloped by waves of anger or fear or sorrow. Their mental function, that part of themselves which helps them process their experience, is used primarily as reflection. This looking back on their experience enables them to observe what happened in the past. From this assessing stance they plan their response to what they decide they have felt.

Magdalene had already written a scenario of her early morning visit to the tomb. She would find someone to remove the stone at the doorway, enter, cleanse and anoint the body, then wrap it in burial cloths. Her grief, instead of engulfing her, was turned to planning and then carrying out the script she had written.

Life, however, provided her with genuine experience. The reality of the situation surprised her so much that she could not take it in. Instead, she tried to substitute her imagined version for the actual one. She decided that the person in whose presence she found herself was a gardener and tried to enlist his help in working out the agenda she had set. As a result, she was blinded to the man before her, the very one who had provided meaning for her life, was Life itself. She perpetuated her limited view of reality rather than let in unimaginable mystery. Lost in her anxious scripts and scenarios, Magdalene abandoned herself. She was compulsively doing in her mind as a preparation for compulsively doing in her outer behavior. She was no longer "in" her experience, but instead was involved in the stimulus/response of compulsive activity.

Maintaining Connections

In relationships, 2/3/4s tend to concentrate on the bond that connects them. They ask: Is it smooth? Is there conflict? Have I made enough overtures to the other that this connection remains intact? Have I let drop those expressions of bonding that testify to "a relationship"? Instinctively, they do not view relationship as one person's presence with another, as being oneself and with someone else. It is as though relationship has an existence in itself; that it is a something, a something that 2/3/4 people often call connection.

Jesus needed to cut through Magdalene's anxiety. Nothing more could happen until he had done so, until he had cleared away the plans she was busily engaged in modifying to fit this change in circumstances. Even before she was aware of the present, Magdalene was on to the future. Before she had perceived what was going on in the moment, she was into decision and action not founded on its reality. Jesus responded to this situation in a way that is helpful to 2/3/4 people. He called Magdalene's name: "Mary!"

It is difficult to describe the effect of being addressed this way for 2/3/4s. It is as though they lose existence to themselves temporarily, forget their own individual person as they plummet into the external world. They need to recall that they have personal parameters, that they exist. Saying their name reminds them that they are. Once they remember they exist, they can reflect on that life. This reflection breaks the driven, anxious plunge into decision and behavior. They pause, turn within, remember themselves. Then they can see other people instead of a collection of things to do in their environment. This is what happened for Magdalene. Jesus' word recalled her to herself. She then was able to recognize his voice and his person standing before her in the here and now.

Having thought long on the next thing Jesus said to Magdalene, I believe it relates once more to the issue of making connections. Apparently Magdalene hung on to Jesus, possibly throwing herself to the ground and grabbing hold of his feet, perhaps folding her arms around his neck as she pressed him to her. Whatever it was that she did, her intent was most likely to ensure their connection. So recently broken by his mysterious behavior and death, it would now be re-established as she had known it. But Jesus called her to another level of being. He told her not to cling to him, and he did so out of love for this woman now purified to the extent of facing her compulsions.

The word *witness* holds what Jesus asked of her. She was now beyond compulsively joining herself with others, something she had always thought was the essence of relationships. Life essentially had been other people for Magdalene, as for other 2/3/4s. Jesus taught her how she was truly to be with others. She must now witness to the presence of Life itself in the world. She had found who she was, and in finding that self she had been opened to a Life beyond and beneath and sustaining. She now knew the Spirit of Jesus because she knew her own spirit.

It was this experience that Jesus asked her to take away and to tell the others about. She was to testify to her own reality. In doing so she would witness to the reality of Jesus still alive. The gospel she was to bring was her own, and yet not merely her own. She would continue to speak the Good News in care and concern for others, but it was good when and only when she opened up and revealed her self in her giving. It was her being present to others that nourished and testified to the Presence that gives Life to all.

How easy this is to say, and how difficult for 2/3/4 people to find in experience. All the world of kindness and concern means nothing without self-knowledge and giving themselves over to genuine emotional reality. Instead, they plot, plan, and adapt themselves to whatever the environment demands so that connections among people can be maintained.

The Mission of Jesus

It must have been a new Magdalene whom the disciples saw when she returned from her errand of mercy, an errand that revealed to her how much mercy she needed to offer herself.

When she told her story now it was not an anxious, rushed one. It was a confident, quiet communication of personal experience. It was her real encounter with Jesus, which made it possible for those she met to have their own experience of Jesus alive.

This was what Magdalene's mission was to the early Christian community. It is the mission of 2/3/4 people to those communities in which they find themselves in these times. They have experienced Life, and they witness what that is for them.

CHAPTER 5

The Story of Thomas

We turn now to Thomas, who embodies the compulsion and trap of the 5/6/7 stance as well as the special gift of people in this space. We see how this disciple's characteristic response is addressed by Jesus, who meets Thomas as he is and who calls him beyond his limitations to a distinctive witness. The mission of Thomas is one that makes use of the uniqueness of his person. It is quite a different mission from that of Magdalene.

A Story of Fear

The disciples on that first day of the week, the day Jesus rose from the dead, were gathered together in a closed room for fear of the Jews. Their leader had met death. Who was to say that they would not be the next ones to be killed? Jesus came to them there, entering despite the closed doors and bringing a message of peace and the strength of the Spirit breathed into each individual. This Spirit gave them power and enabled them to make an informed judgment about sin and forgiveness. From that inspired judgment they could determine whether to forgive or not forgive; they could decide and act.

Thomas, however, was not with them when Jesus came. We do not know where he was or what he was doing. Perhaps even the disciples gathered for purposes of protection and mutual support offered too much togetherness for him. Events of the past few days had at first confused and then appalled

Thomas. He had just lost the man who had promised to provide the answers to his search for meaning in life. Jesus offered the solutions Thomas was looking for—or so he had thought until now. His leader had failed him by failing to impress his accusers with answers to their questions.

Thomas was no longer sure who Jesus was. Perhaps what he had seen as wisdom was emptiness. Perhaps accepting this Jesus and all he promised had been foolish. Whatever was going on, Thomas felt lost. Obviously he had misunderstood Jesus' message. He seems to have needed privacy and time alone to sift through the data of his experience with Jesus, probably going back over it to see where his perceptions had been inaccurate, his conclusions inappropriate.

Ambivalent Anonymity

It may be significant, too, that Thomas was a twin. The anonymity of the 5/6/7 space, the feeling of being of no account to others, undervalued, and even underobserved, takes on significance when we recall that Thomas' entire life had been lived in the company of another person. The moment when an individual marks the beginning of life was not a time for Thomas alone. He had always been accompanied by someone with whom he shared attention. One might wonder whether the assembled disciples had noted Thomas' absence until he rejoined the group. Perhaps only then did they realize he had not had their own experience of Jesus' presence or his Spirit or his call to decision and action. Lost and confused, he may have slipped away by himself unnoticed.

However it happened, Thomas did miss the action of which the others were a part. He had been away from the community. Perhaps he was trying to figure out what had gone on; perhaps he needed an even safer and more private refuge than they could offer in the upper room. How very characteristic of the 5/6/7 person, who often feels that life has passed by while he or she struggled to make sense out of it and fit it into some sort of meaningful perceptual whole. The life that others are inspired by, "moved" by, is something in which 5/6/7s often feel they do not share. Others proceed in life deciding and doing while they stay behind searching for the key that will give them the necessary impetus to act.

The Hyper-Perceptive Stance

Upon his return Thomas is greeted with the story of Jesus' visit. Thomas listens as he is asked to believe what seems impossible to him. How can a dead man have appeared here walking and talking? How could he have come into the room through closed doors? It doesn't make sense; there must be some other explanation for what they say went on. Maybe they had been so grief-stricken that they became suggestible and were led on by the more hysterical members of the group. There must be some logical explanation for all of this. So Thomas did not accept what they said. He listened to their story, but it was one only a fool would believe. This was too significant an event for such superficial reasoning, especially that provided by others who had no authority or claim to knowledge.

Thomas was an honest person. He was not going to pretend that he accepted their account when he did not. He told them he refused to believe what they had said unless he could gather his own data. If this were truly Jesus, then his body would have to be the body of a crucified man. He would have marks of nails in his hands. A soldier had pierced his body. While Thomas had not been standing nearby for that experience, he had probably seen the crucifixion from afar and watched this bystander thrust a lance into Jesus' side to affirm his death. An examination of the alleged physical body of the master he had trusted as the source of his life's meaning would answer questions and resolve issues for him.

Jesus left Thomas in his doubting state for some time. After eight days he returned in much the same way as before: through closed doors and once again speaking a message of peace. This time Thomas was present. Jesus singled him out. Apparently Thomas mattered to him; Thomas seems even to have been the reason for Jesus' return. Jesus apparently knew Thomas well, knew that only data would satisfy him.

Thomas, who lived in the interior world of ideas and insights and perceptual connections, was asked to give the opposite of what Jesus had required of Magdalene. Instead of requesting him to remain with himself alone, untouched and untouching, Jesus asked Thomas to give him his hand. Jesus drew Thomas out of himself. Life in the outer world was what Thomas needed to complete his experience. As Magdalene had to move to her inner life, Thomas had to move outside himself to be in touch with Jesus.

What happened in that moment when Jesus and Thomas met each other in physical contact is not revealed in the gospel passage. Surely something personal and profound took place. It must have been something like an experience of being breathed upon, of receiving Jesus' Spirit, not just as one of the group but personally. Thomas could not deny this special attention of Jesus; he realized that Jesus had come for individuals, had come back to underline that truth especially for Thomas.

Becoming a Believer

Jesus told Thomas he needed to move from doubt to faith. What does this mean for people in the 5/6/7 stance? I think it has to do with moving from merely perceptual to total response. Whereas Thomas was looking for data to substantiate the claims of the other disciples, who attested that Jesus had come and breathed his Spirit into them, he was doing so on a purely perceptual level. Thomas listened to their words but failed to hear their experience. Apparently he missed in them what he also missed in himself: the whole human response of people who had been inspired, inspirited, breathed into, given fullness and life.

Instead of picking up how Jesus alive in the community of believers had touched them, he persisted in looking for objective data he could visually affirm. What Jesus called Thomas to own was his whole life lived affectively and physically. Only by such total living could he become aware of the genuine lives of other people.

Full Human Response

The way for Thomas was to hear the full message of Jesus as given to him. This recalling of Thomas to his own felt experience, his totality of life, involved him in totality of response. He now knew that Jesus was truly present. Jesus was no mere memory. Neither was he a mere intellectual guru or perceptual expert. Jesus was someone who said "Touch me; do not merely look at me. Put your hand into mine. Do not stay over there inside yourself and gather information about me. Know by touch. Feel how much I have given for you, done for you, so that you may live. Know the depth of the wound in my side, which has completely emptied my life blood for your sake."

Thomas did respond and reach out to Jesus. He found that by doing so, his whole person, not merely his perceptual function, became involved. He offered his master a faith that involved heart and body as well as mind. He had thought that all that was asked of him in this life was to find an expert to follow, one to whom he could give allegiance because that person provided the key to life's mystery. In reality, he came to realize that Jesus was more than a man who knew the answers that solved human problems. He was a man whose whole being was filled with commitment to God and to those God had created. He loved all people, but he loved all with a particularity that made him, Thomas, forever and uniquely respected and regarded.

Jesus affirmed those who believe without having to see. But he did not condemn Thomas for being who he was. He accepted him in his need to gather data, dry and dusty though it may have been. He answered Thomas as Thomas needed to be answered: with objective information. Then he surprised him by revealing how much more Spirit and Life there was beyond the perceptual. Jesus gave Thomas himself, his full and loving heart, his body to be touched and eaten and assimilated.

Jesus became the companion who would exemplify the complete human response the Christian mission calls for. He led Thomas out into that frightening world to which Thomas felt he had nothing to offer except his ideas and insights and mental relationships. He drew all of Thomas forth: mind and body, thought and action, awareness and conviction, appraisal and belief. And he did not leave him alone there. He became that inspiration Thomas needed and would continue to need every day of his life.

The gratitude of Thomas burst forth in unaccustomed emotional revelation and response: "My Lord and my God." Those who had seen Jesus only eight days before must have renewed their own commitment. We do not hear that they had expressed their belief at their own time of encounter with the Risen Lord. Thomas, with his need to know all about, to inquire and verify, to substantiate and validate, provided the entire community of disciples with opportunity for faith informed with feeling, considered belief, and experience of the fullness of the message of Christ, which is the presence of Christ.

And Thomas' followers, those people who probe deeply, inquire patiently, and reach out to meet and partake of the person of Jesus, have continued to provide such witness to the Christian community even until now. Such is the special gift of the 5/6/7 stance.

The Story of Peter

We turn now to the third post-resurrection story, the one in which Jesus encounters Peter. This interaction completes a picture of the three basic personalities. Jesus singled out Peter as he had Magdalene and Thomas. He called them, pointed out those compulsions that would interfere with their fullness of life and their contribution to spreading the Good News. He then gave each of them a mission that was congruent with their individual instinct and gift.

A Story of Passion

Peter is a gospel character about whom we know a great deal. Impulsive and impetuous, Peter's raw energy comes through in many incidents when his emotion bursts out in one or another form. He is filled with love and commitment, blind to his limitations, angry at those who do not believe as he believes. He is also terrified and cowardly, repentant and vulnerable, furious and vengeful, overwhelmed with grief. It is this man Jesus calls the rock and upon whom he builds his church. Passionate people like Peter are not always known for their prudence. They are often, however, the kind of people who inspire others and to whom others look for leadership. It is Peter who captures the 8/9/1 instinct, compulsion, and gift.

The story of Jesus' interaction with Peter after the resurrection contains two scenes. The first vignette is the conversation with Peter about commitment and love. The second concerns

Peter's need to surrender, addressing the self-preserving quality
that is basic to this enneagram stance. We will reflect on each
of these scenes in turn, because each underlines a distinct aspect
of 8/9/1 reality.

The Need for Consciousness

The gospel narrative relates that, after eating a meal with the
disciples on the shore of the lake, Jesus engages Peter in what
must have been a private and personal conversation. Peter had
denied Jesus clearly and completely—three times. Jesus calls for
commitment from Peter—just as clearly and completely. Besides the significance of a triple denial, which called for triple
affirmation, there is something here of the 8/9/1 issue of unawareness in the present moment. Peter has already revealed
that he tends not to see and recognize, hear and understand. It
is not Peter who recognizes Jesus standing on the shore while
the disciples are still a distance from land. Rather, it is John
who immediately knows that the one who calls to them across
the water is the Lord.

What is there about Peter, and about 8/9/1s, that makes
them miss what is going on around them in the moment?
Where are they when they are not awake and alert to the
here and now? There may be a number of answers to
these questions. Perhaps Peter was still stunned by the intensity of what had happened during the preceding days. His
promise of fidelity, denial, sorrow, humble penitence, and
dawning awareness of resurrection had swept over him in wave
after wave of feeling. Perhaps he was so exhausted by trying to sustain so many emotional onslaughts that he could
carry on only by holding himself away from and above his
feelings.

Peter did respond to Jesus' repeated questions by stating his
love. What was missing in his original declaration that led Jesus
to ask two more times? The story does not speak of any emotional component to Peter's response until the third time Jesus
placed his question. Was Peter merely giving a perfunctory

answer at first? Was he in some sort of perceptual fog, which left him somehow wandering in a state of unawareness?

The events of the previous days could well have left Peter much like a beached whale, worn out with struggling against adverse elements. He might well have chosen, consciously or unconsciously, to remain disengaged from life until he could find the energy to move on from this intense period. Jesus, however, continued to ask for commitment, continued to require engagement. Did not Peter deserve some rest after all he had been through? Jesus apparently did not think so. Not only was Peter to be interiorly faithful, but that inner pledge was also to be expressed in care and concern and nourishment of others. Peter was to be a shepherd, Jesus told him. Appealing to him in such an image must have shown Peter that he was called to tend with conscious and consistent care the flock Jesus would leave to him as his responsibility.

But why now, when Peter was so emotionally spent, was he being asked for more? Why not let him recuperate and be refreshed? We have no answer to this, but we know that Jesus persisted in his questioning. He demanded integrity from Peter: inner and outer congruence. Eventually, after three attempts, he engaged Peter emotionally and Peter's profession of fidelity and love became passionately conscious.

Jesus chose at this point to underline what Peter would be asked to do as his life moved on. Until now, Peter had made his own decisions. Now he was to follow the flow of life which would sometimes require decision and action he would prefer to avoid. Peter was told, again in an image, that he was to stretch out his hands to be bound and led where he would rather not travel.

Many times in future years Peter was to live out this symbolic surrender in the real events of his life. His confrontations with the early church led him to reverse his judgments and demands that converts adopt the rituals and customs of Judaism. Finally, after a life of docility to the Spirit of Jesus expressed in the early Christian community, Peter was literally imprisoned and martyred. By the time of his death, Peter must have learned very well what surrender is all about.

Just a word here about the way Jesus chose to present Peter with his mission. Images and symbols are of special significance to people in the 8/9/1 stance. Their thinking is primarily analogical. Experience is best described as being similar to something else. Metaphors such as shepherd and sheep, or being held captive, convey not only factual information but also emotional content. Such images capture levels of meaning 8/9/1s find helpful. These word pictures engage their attention and energy and involve them affectively.

In efforts to feel in control of their emotional lives, 8/9/1s will sometimes use logic and analysis as a cover for intense feeling. Without the emotional component, however, 8/9/1s experience none of the energy needed to engage them in committed response to life's demands. Addressing reality in imagery and symbol retains the emotional element so instinctive for people in this space. As a result of choosing an affective approach to understanding, perception becomes clear and the heart inspired.

The call to shepherd lambs and sheep and to be bound by one more powerful than he called forth unselfish love from the previously undisciplined Peter. Interiorly and exteriorly blown on the wings of emotional impulse, Peter is asked to move beyond what he likes and dislikes to an informed, selfless dedication. This response is not less passionate than before, but now accurate perception and informed commitment have extended it to include others' needs and nourishment. Jesus knew how to say what Peter needed to and was able to hear.

Call to Surrender

There was one other defense that Peter tried against Jesus. He had, however grudgingly, seemed to accept the need for selfless energy in compassionate service for those entrusted to the master. He was asked as well for surrender and a willingness to be led to situations in which he might not win or be powerful. Fear had been evident in Peter's recent outright denial of a Jesus pushed around, judged, and manipulated by leaders and people. Now he was being asked for his own surrender to what could well turn out to be the same sort of powerlessness. Peter held his own ground until completely convinced that Jesus was neither enemy nor imposter. He knew that to remain Jesus' friend he must agree to what Jesus asked. He knew he had to say yes in order to retain any self-respect.

Since so much had been asked of him, Peter wanted to make sure that he was not the only one who had to sacrifice himself for Jesus. There were other disciples besides Peter. In particular, there was John, whom he turned to look at even as he and Jesus talked. John had been following behind the two of them. Obviously, John was also a favored disciple, another one with whom Jesus shared intimately. What would John have to hand over as his price for friendship with Jesus? What would Jesus ask of this other man, so loved, so much a part of all that had gone on the past few days? Peter felt he was entitled to know.

Jesus addressed this last resistance in Peter, not by attending to his question, but by insisting that Peter look at his own personal call. It was not Peter's place, Jesus reminded him, to make sure that commitment and challenge would be equally measured out. What did it matter to Peter, Jesus wanted to know, what kind of sacrifice John would be asked for?

Peter was probably not asking about John in order to compare the two of them. He knew Jesus loved both of them. He had no tendency to measure affective response quantitatively. Peter knew very well that feelings for different people defied comparison. What, then, was Peter asking Jesus? He may have wanted to know how much energy John would need to expend, what sacrifice John would have to promise. How much comfort must John give up and how much commitment must John have? Would he be asked for personal surrender as costly as Peter's own?

If Peter were to be required to give Jesus everything and

follow him wherever he led, then John should have to pay as
great a price. Both of them ought to be asked to give up self-
concern and comfort. That, after all, was what justice meant:
equal gain for equal pain.

Jesus merely put aside Peter's questioning complaint and repeated his statement requiring personal surrender. "You are to
follow me," Jesus said. Whatever Jesus might ask of John was
to be no concern of Peter's. The argument was irrelevant; Jesus
rested his case and Peter saw still another time that he was dealing with someone whom his objections could not distract or
deter. There was no possible way Peter could hold out even a
small corner for himself and his interests.

It is not an easy matter for 8/9/1 persons to give up their
own territory, whether psychic or physical, with its comforts,
ease, and satisfactions. Once having done so, however, affective
involvement with others inspires trust and commitment from
those for whom they care. In turn, they lovingly respond to
others' needs. People in this stance can become the best of
those who serve. They do so by encouraging others to utilize
their own personal resources.

People in the 8/9/1 stance will always be aware of their individual parameters and those of other people. They will no
longer need either to merge with the ones they love or build
up barriers to assure themselves existence. Instead, they will encourage independent resourcefulness in those they help. These
people may be weak and vulnerable to political suppression
and servitude, physical and psychological poverty. People who
are 8/9/1s help others take their first steps to finding strength
for themselves. They then encourage these others to develop
their powers even further. A better life follows when boundaries dissolve between people, and unity becomes something
real.

The price 8/9/1 people pay for their contribution is nothing less than selfless toil. It is true commitment they give,
because once dedicated there is no turning back, no neglect,
no disengagement. They are, indeed, worn out in the cause

of justice. In their own passionate commitment they alleviate the sufferings of others who have no power or strength and show them how and where to find their own energy. This is their gift to the people of God; this is their yes to the call to follow Jesus.

CHAPTER 7

The Meaning of Incarnation

Enneagram theory states that each aspect of creation reflects something of the Divine. To say this in Christian theological terms, each of the three basic enneagram stances reflects a person of the Trinity.[1] Another way to put this is that the gift of each stance makes present in this world one of the Divine Persons. God is manifested in each of us but not fully in any one of us. Our enneagram space indicates what Divine aspect is most ours.

When we talked about virtue and vice, we noted that these are two sides of the same coin; our gift exaggerated into compulsion is our vice. We also spoke about the attempt to eliminate our vice, which is not the way to approach conversion. Even if we were able to stamp out our vice, we would lose our gift in the process of doing so. We are called to choose life; the day-to-day of living purifies us. It shows us to ourselves as we really are rather than how we imagine ourselves to be. Our observations and those of others are what lead us to admit our reality, our personal truth. Then conversion happens.

It follows that when we find the gift of reflecting a Divine Person in ourselves, we will also see that gift exaggerated into compulsion. We tend to distort the word we are in efforts to improve on whom God has created. We will look now at both that giftedness and the distortion of it to which we tend as these relate to Creator, Son, and Spirit.

Those Who Reflect the Spirit of Jesus

After his resurrection from the dead, Jesus breathed his Spirit into his disciples gathered in the upper room. Then he offered them peace and went away. He left the world of time and space, but he did not leave it an orphaned world. His Spirit was breathed into people for all time to come. God in each age is known through human beings who carry the Spirit of Jesus and that Spirit's energy in their own energetic spirit.

The 2/3/4 people in a special way experience as well as witness to Christ's Spirit alive here and now. One might say they are people of Christian community. The bonds that link people together are their focus; these bonds take up their time and energy. Networking among people makes for life and meaning.

Teaching in other countries has demonstrated to me that every culture includes a reasonably balanced number of people in all nine enneagram spaces. We have Peter, Thomas, and Magdalene as well as many other gospel personalities to hint that the community of Jesus' first followers was also cosmopolitan. We might expect that to be so. Nevertheless, the behaviors of this early community as recounted in Acts 1 and 2 do demonstrate some of the characteristics of 2/3/4s. Perhaps it would be more accurate to say that Luke, through whose eyes we see this community, appears to have a 2/3/4 stance. At any rate, as we look now at these disciples in the time from Jesus' return to the Father and the sending of his Spirit to be with them, we observe some 2/3/4 issues.

Luke tells us the disciples gathered in an upper room after they returned to the city from the Mount of Jesus' ascension. They remained there several days in constant prayer. Jesus their leader was gone, and they seemed to have no idea what to do next. Situations without direction or plan are laced with anxiety for 2/3/4s. When disruptions in their lives throw them off center and they are without specific goals and defined roles, 2/3/4s find it hard to be still. Often they make up job descriptions for themselves to order their lives in security. That is just what the disciples did. They called a meeting of sorts, nominated candidates to replace Judas the betrayer, and chose Matthias for that position.

Herein we find one of the traps of 2/3/4 people. They can become engrossed in group functioning and busy themselves with meetings to shape and control the environment. When distant from their affective life they look for something to do and often choose to do that something with others. They assemble people to determine and carry out tasks the group has set.

In their emptiness and loss the disciples found support by discussing and resolving specific needs. They knew they were not adequate to carry out Jesus' mission. When he was leaving them, Jesus had predicted they would receive power from the Spirit and witness to him throughout the world. Responsibility had been given, but inner strength had not. Rather than wait for energy, they busied themselves with whatever tasks seemed immediate. Waiting for the sense of readiness becomes an impossible task for people who have lost touch with inner clues about interior reality and the feeling of right and wrong. They are thrust into action without such clues.

Then, on Pentecost, power came. The Spirit descended, not on the group as a whole, says Luke, but on the head of each of them as a tongue of fire. It was not the group as a group that was inspired; it was the individuals. These individuals experienced life within them. Now they had that sense of readiness, and it empowered them as it gave direction to their mission. Each one knew that energy, something that individual flames seem to symbolize. By speaking their personal message the disciples, like Magdalene, testified to Life beyond their lives, Spirit beyond their spirit. Like Magdalene, who was a compelling witness to truth when she came to know herself, these inspirited disciples became understood by their listeners. Even language barriers dissolved, Luke tells us. It must have been a surprised community spreading the Spirit on Pentecost. Surely it was a busy one, but the activity was no longer busyness. It had become centered and directed.

What the gathered group had known as their own empty, unfocused lives became infused suddenly with Life that commanded response. The message went forth from their mouths. They let it go. The rest was up to the hearers. Their spirited example gave courage to their listeners, who responded in astonishing numbers, about three thousand that day. Their spirits, empowered by the Spirit now united to them, encountered others open to the gospel of Jesus. They were from that day on not just a group, but a community of believers.

Luke's story in the Acts of the Apostles tells how the church was born. It also tells how people of the church carry the Good News to others as the flames of affective fervor in the messengers ignite ready material into flames of affective fervor in others. In this way Jesus' prophecy of witness throughout the world becomes actuality. The Spirit fills the earth, breathing at will. People of the church are instruments of that Spirit.

> We seem to sense that—whether we conceive it as a divine being or as cosmic energy—the Spirit working upon and within all creation is shaping it into order, harmony, and beauty, uniting all beings (some willing but the majority as yet blind and rebellious) with each other through links of love, achieving—slowly and silently, but powerfully and irresistibly—the Supreme Synthesis.[2]

Thus the psychologist Roberto Assagioli expresses how divine energy manifests itself in the world.

For 2/3/4s the emphasis in spirituality comes from the side of humanity. That the human person is godly becomes the astonishing consideration—even more so, experience—of 2/3/4s. The spirituality of 2/3/4s is a horizontal one. There is no inclination to look toward the heavens to find the Divine. One only need turn to one's own heart and the hearts of others to find life/Life and spirit/Spirit. That spirit/Spirit is alive in the world because the community of faithful disciples is alive. They enflesh this Spirit in their own flesh as they gather in Jesus' name.

Those Who Reflect the Son of God

There is for all of us a need to grow from infancy through all the stages of life into ever greater maturity. We have many memories about the price of moving out to be ourselves. These memories hold the emotions we instinctively turn to in crises, those of safety, security, and power. For some, it is *fear* that surfaces thoughts of losing a Paradise of complete protection. Others view stepping out and leaving the Garden behind as a necessary though *anxious* move. Still others brace themselves against a powerful world beyond that early Eden, *standing strong* in the face of adversaries.

How do we arrive at a place of submission to Providence or fate or creatureliness or a loving Creator or however we look at the Life Force that leads us where we must follow? How do we become that separate individual who can take charge of life and its decisions? And finally, how do we balance submission and personal authority? We all ask these questions, no matter where we may be on the enneagram circle. But 5/6/7s experience this struggle between docility and freedom with the greatest intensity. It is facing this issue that incarnates them as children of God who, like Jesus, speak from personal authority even as they obey the Father's will.

The dynamic for 5/6/7 people, more than for any others, is that of owning choice and responsibility while remaining a loving and teachable child of someone wiser and more experienced. Especially in adolescence we see this struggle. Most of us remember our own teenage years and watch today's teens enact their own drama of growing individuality. The seesaw of rebellion to dependence is part of this scenario. People from other spaces on the enneagram struggle less to resolve this issue. For 5/6/7s, however, putting to rest this developmental concern is not so easy. It is one that will probably stay with them a time.

There is something of the child that 5/6/7 people never seem to lose. Often their faces, even in old age, look youthful.

Their naive belief in others' honesty, their literal interpretation of people's words, have a quality of childlike trust. Often children in these spaces maintain subservience to adults longer than people from other stances do. The safety of the family circle, not needing to stand out in verbal or nonverbal self-revelation, makes childhood desirable, and so they tend to prolong it.

When they do venture out to independent decision and action, 5/6/7s find such forays terrifying; the outer world is not a place where they are at ease and comfortable. Others in it function more efficiently than they do. Conscious effort of leaping or rushing or pushing out is costly for people in this space. It is often followed by a frightened withdrawal to safety and submission, purchased at the price of independence. Neither of these movements flows naturally; they show the self-consciousness of difficult decision coming from perception rather than from the whole person.

A number of gospel characters demonstrate aspects of this swing from anonymity to assertion, from docility to independence. One is the woman who had a hemorrhage for twelve years (Lk 8:43–48). She had tried every treatment and had finally determined to approach Jesus with her need. But the crowds were large, and she saw her decision to state her problem as insignificant in the face of the multitudes. She may have been following Jesus around for some time. We can't know that. We do know, however, that she decided to remain anonymous even from him she so admired and trusted.

In her fear she reached out, unknown to anyone, unseen by the crowd. Her faith saved her and she was cured, though still anonymously. Jesus felt power leaving his person. Entering into her body, this power cured her and made her strong. Jesus chose to acknowledge this change in her, publicly attesting that it partook of his own. He announced her health to his bystanders. As he did so she realized her own importance and the power it gave.

Another disciple who was at first reluctant to follow Jesus, then afterward eagerly proclaimed his faith, was Nathaniel, one of the first companions Jesus chose to announce his Good News (Jn 1:44–51). Nathaniel, an Israelite in whom there was no deceit, seems to have been a straightforward sort of man. Like Thomas, he wanted proof of Jesus as the Messiah. Jesus had not yet publicly declared himself the Promised One, but neither had he denied it when others saw him in that role. Nathaniel remained skeptical until he could appraise things for himself. He approached Jesus, and when Jesus was introduced to him, Nathaniel was amazed to hear Jesus say that he had seen Nathaniel underneath the fig tree even before their meeting.

From a place of withdrawal and doubt, Nathaniel leapt out in an act of faith. Jesus promised even more wonders than this rather simple one, which impressed Nathaniel so much. Maybe Jesus had uncovered some private interior struggle or significant action of Nathaniel's to the wonder of this disciple. Once Nathaniel knew Jesus was aware of him in his private moments, he submitted to this prophet who knew all about him. Nathaniel had wanted to see Jesus and evaluate him; he found instead that he was seen by Jesus and that the master had read his open and naked heart.

Another person who demonstrates the patience to live without results, an attitude characteristic of 5/6/7s, is the paralytic at the Pool of Bethesda (Jn 5:1–16). For thirty-eight years, the story tells us, this man had considered the possibility of being able to do normal things. He had imagined that somebody would come along and make it happen for him, but so far nobody had. Then Jesus saw him, singled him out, heard his need. Jesus did not carry him to the pool. Instead, he told him to stand up and walk. The paralytic felt strength in his body and, because of his faith in this man, found himself able to make things happen for himself.

The trap for 5/6/7 people is to remain stuck inside themselves, avoiding putting outside who they are and how they believe. The demand to live up to beliefs is postponed until certainty can be reached. Search for absolute sureness can become a refuge, an excuse to stay in safety instead of emerging in personal authority and responsibility for actions consonant with beliefs.

Like all people who move to maturity, the time comes when 5/6/7s must stand on their own feet, whatever that image may mean for them. It may be affirmation of religious beliefs or values. It may be dedication to some person or group. It may be acting on what is important for their personal life. Whatever standing alone and visible, accepting responsibilities of decision and action or revealing to others what matters to them might mean, it can happen only with the experience of energy and power.

Like the woman with the hemorrhage, the disciple Nathaniel, and the paralytic, 5/6/7 people experience as they grow to self that surge of energy that calls them out to follow Jesus. With him they proclaim the good news of salvation: Belief asks for personal commitment and action. Faith is more than perceptual confirmation. It is an energy that comes from the heart. It transforms the jerky, back-and-forth darting out and withdrawing of 5/6/7s to a consistent flow of life-giving and life-receiving energy.

Jesus is not merely a model for 5/6/7s. He is the one who inspires. Jesus does more than provide an example of an autonomous person voluntarily choosing submission to the profound authority of Life itself. He fills others with that very life. Those who look to him for testimony find a Life and Love that calls forth their own emotionally inspired and heartfelt commitment. It is not that people in this stance are to behave as Jesus behaved in gospel times. Rather, they are to live their lives, as Carl Jung has said, as fully as Jesus lived his life.

Tradition is important for 5/6/7s. The past has much to teach about living here and now. But what traditions have most to offer are not particulars of living or transplanting decisions from one generation to another. The spirit of the law must be clung to, as the spirit of Jesus, God's obedient and free Son, is clung to. Tradition with its laws and rules and parameters may look very different when applied to current circumstances. But that does not matter. The spirit of the law, its heart and intent and reason for being, will endure.

Jesus acted and spoke about just this reality when he did away with the Old Law of the former Testament, not by replacing it but fulfilling it with the New Law of the gospel. A system of meaning and value based on belief and hope and love is never out of date, even though it may look radically different from one age to the next. The person who lives out that meaning is as ever-changing as the system, while ever rooted in truth as Jesus was.

What every child—and especially every 5/6/7 growing to maturity—must learn is that being adult is neither rebellion from all that parents stand for nor adopting their values without assessing what is fitting. Being an adult is becoming our own person, imbibing the life from the past and expressing it in an individual way. This is how we move from being children of our parents to being adult sons and daughters. That equality of relationship makes children collaborators with father and mother, sharing as Adam and Eve shared in God's friendship as they walked together in the Garden. It is recovering once again, but only after rebellion has taken place and personal freedom been asserted, the respect and reverence for self and parent that makes for balance and wholeness.

The lesson so important for 5/6/7 people is that God became a human being, testifying to respect for the human condition. Every creator, human or Divine, longs to have another to love and cherish. It is the flowering of that care that results in respect for the freedom of the other. Parent reverences son and daughter; child reverences parent. This mature interdependence is what 5/6/7s need to experience. It strengthens them to live their own free lives.

Those Who Reflect the Creator God

One aspect of the God we consider to be Trinity is that of Life-giver and Nourisher. The Source of Existence who sends forth a God Son out of love and who leaves his personal

Spirit among creatures for all times and places is often the first image of God we experience. We look to our parents for all we need: food, shelter, comfort, attention. Without their concern, as without the sustaining concern of the Creator, we cannot survive. We learn very early that we are dependent on someone more powerful than we are, someone who must constantly hold us in mind or we will cease to be.

One of our early learnings is that those who represent Life for us at some point fail us. At the very least they disappoint us; at most, they reject or abandon us. We lose confidence in the gods of our lives and become our own provider, surviving as well as we can. We determine no longer to fall back into illusion of another's loving care.

We all know such an experience, because we have all committed that fundamental sin leading us to choose survival at the price of loneliness and isolation. But it is 8/9/1 people who especially experience themselves as being cast aside and uncared for. They, more than any others on the enneagram circle, concern themselves with preserving and providing strength and nourishment from whatever source they can find, within themselves or in their environment.

Loss of Paradise, the place of the "care-full" God/parent, angers 8/9/1s. They resent the deception of their parents' unfulfilled promise and determine never to be seduced again. The message they take in and tell themselves is one of personal dismissal. They grow up "care-less" of themselves and others. The world is a careless place; like Jeremiah they have been duped and they have let themselves be duped. They resolve that they never will be again.

The journey to self, which is the journey to that place where we come to know the genuine Creator who authored us, is the path of surrender to Someone we come to know as merciful, forgiving, and loving. As we learn to embrace and care for ourselves later in life, we live more and more from that place where we also know the embrace and care of the Divine. For 8/9/1s, this journey involves tests of will and strength, struggles between capitulation and resistance. It becomes a choice between holding out to claim power and returning to that absorbing, merging, undifferentiated time of infancy and Paradise. In this Garden of Eden, which preceded separation and sinfulness, they are freed from efforts to become unique, separate beings.

More than any other people 8/9/1s remember this Paradise and want it back again. More than others they go back and forth from thinking it was only a dream and hiding once again in its comforts. From being independent—if unsatisfying—nourishers of themselves, 8/9/1s fall back into blending their individual existence with that of people they come to trust, much as they once did their parents in that Paradise before choice and separation. Boundaries between their own being and another's being dissolve. More than any other stance on the enneagram, 8/9/1s keep searching for Someone to provide for them. In efforts to find the True God, they become alternately parent/nourishers for themselves and others, and people who hide their face in unconsidered repose at the breast of whomever they see filling their needs.

As they struggle to preserve and conserve themselves, 8/9/1s alternate in compulsion between unquestioning, demanding comfort and vengeful, punishing reprisal. At times they may be champions of those who seem to have no power, imitating the all-providing quality of God. At other times they may forget others as they sink back into their own experience of infancy, when they accepted care without responsibility.

Sometimes they act as though everything in their own and others' lives depends on their struggle for justice and equality. Sometimes they forget about others as they reach out for their own satisfaction. Like a child lovingly embracing a teddy bear one moment and casting it away for something more immediate, 8/9/1s in their compulsive state put others aside in much the same way they feel they were put aside. They become limited caretakers similar to their own parents.

We have already seen how Jesus demanded consistent commitment from Peter. We look now at the Old Testament character of Jacob who was called to wrestle with someone he did not recognize (Gn 32:23–32). Jacob was on his way to a reconciliation meeting with his brother Esau when he found himself left alone for the night. In that aloneness he became engaged in a wrestling match with a powerful stranger. The battle lasted until morning; there was no respite for Jacob. The two seemed to have gotten acquainted in the very act of pushing against one another. Jacob discovered his own strength and power, his personal boundaries, and in his struggle defined himself.

The One-Who-Fought asked Jacob his name and then changed it to Israel, which means "strong against God." He was promised that he would be strong against humans, too. This One-Who-Fought refused to submit to Jacob's request that he reveal his name, but the experience itself had taught Jacob the identity of his antagonist. Jacob not only discovered who he was; he found out that his efforts to defend himself had outlined for him the face of God.

The Strong-One-in-Battle was Jacob's antagonist. God revealed identity in the struggle so that Jacob knew he could never hold out against so formidable an opponent. In order that Jacob would never forget this occasion, the One-Who-Fought left him wounded and vulnerable. A lasting limp would recall to Jacob both his limitations and the reality that there was someone he could never overcome. Jacob, like Peter, learned that the only intelligent course of action was surrender to God. And God never let Jacob forget it, as he allowed him to limp through his future.

This God who is the Source and Sustainer of Life is the God Moses met at Mount Horeb (Ex 3:1–15). Tending his father-in-law's sheep one day, Moses noticed a blazing fire in the middle of a bush. It was a fire that did not destroy. Moses approached closer, but God in the bush warned Moses to stay where he was. Moses had to keep his own boundary and territory and reverence the bush as holy ground. On this spot, Moses in his own space and God in God's, the Divine

Fire chose to be revealed as Being without cause or effect or explanation.

God ordered Moses to go forth and bring the people to a land that would be their own when they were delivered from bondage and injustice. Moses did not want to do this work God assigned him, and he asked again and again how such a thing would be possible. In response, God promised to be with him as the one who not only sent but supported. Moses was to witness to the Eternal Other as messenger. Again we see God demanding sacrifice, sending a deliverer to the people and revealing Divinity as Being itself.

This Creator God takes the name of Source of Existence. It is this God we think we have found in the early days of life when we live in the Paradise of parental attention and care. Life unfolds for us the lesson of early disappointment and independent determination which carries us through years of experience. Eventually, if we are truly contemplative and awake to our ever-changing reality, we learn our deepest word and find therein that true Source of Life, nearer to us than we are to ourselves. This is the journey for everybody, but it takes on special significance for 8/9/1s. Like Moses, their issues are around surrender to this One who calls for obedience and reverence, who is both loving God and powerful adversary. When Moses hesitates to follow this God of Being, Yahweh comes to meet him and tries to kill him. Moses is saved by his wife's intercession, and Yahweh lets him live and urges him to set his people free. Moses, like Peter and Jacob, learns the power of God and his own powerlessness before Divinity.

The trap of the 8/9/1 stance is to swing back and forth from the inner world to the outer. It takes effort to remain alert in the present moment, neither forgetting past experience contained therein nor overlooking the future this present foreshadows. The perspective that attention to past, present, and future can give is often lost to 8/9/1 people. Not only is this connection of time problematic, but other perceptual connections fail to signal full reality as one experience relates to another.

When 8/9/1 people become fixed in their interior world, the external environment and people in it suffer either behavioral or emotional neglect. When 8/9/1s are locked in the outer world and its struggles and issues, they forget about their interior journey. Beyond these opposites of inner and outer, 8/9/1s do well to remind themselves of other polarities. Alongside doubt and fear and despair and hatred exist faith and courage and hope and love. The perceptual function allows inner and outer and polar opposites of feeling to be together. Both blinding emotion and repressing blinding emotion prevent 8/9/1s from seeing and hearing their complete experience.

Some sort of activity often helps people in this stance. Whether talking or writing or exercising or working in graphic arts, doing something can bring their minds and hearts together. Perception needs to be added to their experience. It provides context and relates various parts of reality to one another. It offers a meaningful configuration to discrete bits of life. Besides being affective, they become affectively present. Eyes and ears join heart in the approach to the moment. They are awake and alert in the now.

Such consciousness empowers both 8/9/1s and those who are nourished by it. Responsibility for self leads them to inspire responsibility in others. Besides being life-givers and nourishers for themselves, they empower others to be so in their own lives. Instead of resenting and rebelling against the loss of parent/providers, they own their own selves, where the genuine Source of Nourishment resides. They do not neglect or punish themselves any longer, nor do they neglect and punish other people.

The result of self-care and self-nourishment is a world of individual people who are no longer at war with one another. Having passed beyond the instinctual judgment of like or dislike, an attitude on which children base care, they move into selfless expenditure of energy that others might live. They do not live in others or for them but together with them. The relationship Jesus revealed in his prayer to the Father at the Last Supper outlines the mature existence 8/9/1s struggle to find—Jesus and his Father are one and yet separate persons. All others are to be one as they are. Each person is to remain an individual but united in all-embracing love and selfless concern.

The Language of Mysticism

The depth of incarnation, an incarnation that unites us with Jesus also enfleshed in a human body, has been expressed by holy people in many ways. All mystery invites attempts at articulation, even though words forever fall short. The mystery of incarnation has challenged writers and led to the accusation of pantheism for some of them. How is it that the Divine Being enters into creation? Julian of Norwich said that between God and the soul there is no between. This is a reflection of Augustine of Hippo's declaration that God is nearer to us than we are to ourselves.

Are these people saying that we created beings are God? I think not. Rather, they seem to be affirming that the core of the human personality, what Jung calls the self, is where one experiences the Divine. The more one lives from this center—and living from the center is the second task of life—the closer is the Life and Spirit beyond it. Thomas Merton called this personal reality the true self. He adds that when one lives in such a way, one cannot but know Being greater than the self. An image which might be helpful in this regard is one of "falling beneath" the center, one's unique, individual boundary, into Fullness of Being, the author of one's own being.[3]

Participation in a Life beyond life would seem to be what transcendental psychologists and mystics alike are talking about. Jesus himself struggled to speak about this reality, which he experienced and asked his Father to give his followers: "May they be one in us, as you are in me and I am in you . . . that they may be one as we are one. With me in them and you in me" (Jn 17:21–23, JB).

Now let us listen to some everyday mystics say much the same thing about their own experience of God.

I like walking by the lake. Sometimes I have the feeling that
the water and the gulls and the clouds and the sand under
my feet and me, too, are all somehow part of the Divine
Life.

Another person who lives in a large city puts it this way:

I ride the bus to work every morning. That's become like
a prayer time for me. I just look around at all those people
sitting there reading or sleeping or standing up holding on
to the overhead straps. We're packed in like sardines. I just
keep saying over and over inside: "This is God, this is God."

As we continue into the second task of our lives, we become
increasingly aware of how profound the doctrine of the Divine
becoming one with humanity is.

Other persons may look at incarnation from a different emphasis, even from the opposite side.

When I think of what it means that God became a human
being, I'm in awe of what this is about for people. There's
that old image of a wonderful exchange when God becomes
human so we can become godly. Each one of us is so significant. I like to remind myself of that fact.

For some it is the person of Jesus who inspires to courage and
action.

The story of Jesus driving the moneychangers out of the
temple has always intrigued and sort of scared me. He knew
he had to stand up for what he realized was his Father's
honor. So he did. He took the bull by the horns, even though
he must have been afraid of what they would do to him. I
know I have to do that same thing in my life, however that
comes about.

Others need to arrive at that perspective which makes their
individual pieces of reality into a whole. Each part of their
existence finds its place in relationship to the rest.

I stood out under the stars last night. All of a sudden everything fell into place. I could see that all my flailing around
and fighting the air was childish. There's a loving Somebody
out there that cares for me and Dan, and the whole darn
creation, too. That Somebody gathers us up all together in
loving arms.

Surrender to a God who holds power and who is trustworthy
helps some people to be aware of interior, personal skills and
their consequent responsibilities.

I live near the ocean. My favorite thing when I'm feeling
blown away or totally flat and bored—my other-side feeling
from blown away—is to stand on the shore and watch the
waves come up just so far, just to my toes. They'll never
wash me away because I have it in my power to move out
of their path. They can come up close and even touch me,
but they don't have to drown me. I can choose to stay just
out of their grasp, moving back a little bit as the tide comes
in closer and closer. That makes me feel very peaceful and
in control of myself. I know I can make it no matter how
strong my feelings get to be.

Images of Coming to Wholeness

People who are 2/3/4s do not look outside to find God,
but into themselves. Doing so fits best with their innate gesture
toward life. They have energy that instinctively and often compulsively draws them outward. To come to balance they need
to move inward. Images of nest or vessel or cup or inner home
are common. This symbolic language from the unconscious
makes a statement about the center and heart where peace and
life and energy reside. They need to reflect and find that heart
place where Life, that energetic Spirit frequently referred to
as God, dwells. When 2/3/4s arrive at some realization of the
importance of movement within to self-presence, they tend to
see themselves as merely secular. There must be more to a God
experience than this feeling of "at home." This cannot be all
there is; this is so human. It is merely an experience of one's

self. Yes, it is. And such an experience is precisely their call to
wholeness.

It is necessary for 5/6/7s to move outside themselves to find
balance and centeredness. It is in the outer environment where
they touch and taste and smell and listen to and talk with and
embrace and push against that they find the aspect of God they
need in order to fill up what is wanting in themselves. The
image of journeying, so common in these times of renewed
spirituality, is especially important for 5/6/7s. They need to
open the doors of their inner home and go out to other people
who will speak to them the wonders of God.

It is important for 5/6/7s to remember that a journey made
in slow and consistent segments is the kind that will conserve
their strength. Running hard one day to catch up for a yesterday spent sitting around poring over maps does not provide
the steady, regular, consistent covering of step by step, day
by day. Conserving resources and meting them out little by
little rather than in stops and starts is the way of a seasoned
traveler.

There is something of coming to know the adversary and his
power and skill and strength that is necessary for 8/9/1s. One
can only find out the dimensions of God's face by pressing
against the Divine features in the circumstances and people one
encounters in life. One can only know oneself, as well, through
one's response in the battles of life. Where is one's power and
strength to be assessed if not by pitting oneself against powerful
forces?

The spiritual image for 8/9/1s is that of yielding to a Being
who is clearly in charge. Such yielding is not that kind of surrender that forces one to be locked into some prison camp, but
one in which a person finds that the supposed adversary is really
seeking to combine forces in mutual efforts for justice. Often
the image of moving one's hand on the rudder of a sailboat in
order to join personal energy with that of the wind provides
helpful pondering for 8/9/1s. Both sailor and wind combine
to move the boat toward its destination. If this cooperation of

energy does not take place, the boat is at best without direction and at worst capsized.

Images From Dreams

Life becomes no longer a struggle, a problem, a task; it is being who one truly is. And this can be the human experience found anywhere, any time. More and more human beings dare to venture into becoming more fully themselves, but now from the center of their being. Von Durckheim says:

> Divine Being is beyond all opposites. It is undoubtedly present within us, but it cannot flourish in this life of ours if, ignoring the multiform and conflicting aspects of the world, we remove ourselves from the market place and dwell in a place apart. Man can only grow from the root of essential Being when he allows even those things that are repugnant to approach him. He must without reservation confront the powers of the world just as they are, neither avoiding the dark, nor lingering in the light. It is only by freely and repeatedly choosing new encounters, by marching on and, when necessary, yielding up that which has been most dearly bought, that the skin, so to speak, of the inner man (which is necessary for his survival in the world) can grow strong, and the instruments needed for the building of a new, more valid structure be tempered and given a cutting edge.[4]

This same reality Von Durckheim describes is often expressed in symbolic language from the unconscious.

> I sometimes dream about a room inside me where I can go to relax. I'm there with my friend John. We lie on top of the blue bedspread together and we talk. I feel like I've spent a quiet, intimate time in my very private home. I wake up refreshed from these dreams.

Another person who has different dynamics might dream something else.

> I have a favorite dream that always makes me laugh when I wake up. I'm fingerpainting with a classroom of preschoolers.

We're covered with the stuff and the paper is wet and slimy. Everybody's having a great time. Somebody turns to me and starts painting my face. I'm hesitant, but then I begin to do the same thing. Pretty soon we're all up to our elbows in paint and smearing it all over everybody else.

Still another dream captures the resolution of different issues:

I'm tied up in a prison cell. Then there's an earthquake and all the doors spring open. Reminds me of St. Peter when he was in prison. I run out screaming and hollering and I notice that there are a lot of other prisoners who have been sprung the same way I have. We start running down a road that ends at a cliff. I look down and see water. Then I realize we're on Alcatraz Island. We want to get out of this place, but the scene is bedlam. I climb up on a big rock and begin to give out orders to the bunch of them after I quiet them down. I tell them we can do it if we just work together. They listen and begin to do what I say. I'm sure we'll escape all right.

Peace and inner richness as well as energy for the day's work come from living out of this center of life/Life. The experience is one of privacy and yet companionship. People are with themselves when they touch into this place of self. And this is a self who cares for and loves them, rather than one who criticizes and judges them. Individuals are more than limited, needy beings in this place. A Greater-Than-Self is there, too.

How can human beings hope to be in God's presence and know God in this world other than through the nature God has given them? It is mind, affections, and body that mediate Fullness of Life to sharers in that Fullness. Whether we eat or drink, whatever we are doing, St. Paul says, we do all for the glory of God, that Life in which we participate (1 Cor 10:31).

But the questions keep coming. Isn't there more to the spiritual life? Can I be sure I'm praying? Shouldn't I be more pious? How can these ordinary things like taking care of the children or driving the car or working at my desk be spiritual? Perhaps the answers to these questions are other questions. Just who is God anyway? How can we know God? Can God be expressed in the energy that fills us and yet leaves us present to ourselves? Can God be in life-giving relationships? If God is Life and Energy, if God is present in this world today, how better can we know that God than through our daily, centered being and doing?

Human Wholeness Is Spirituality

It all seems so human, this finding God in everyday living. God is everywhere. God is in the scriptures—and the music and the liturgy and the novel and the daily paper. God is also in everything else, including all of the people who cross our path each day and are allowed to share our centeredness beneath that false centeredness in perception, emotion, and activity we tried to create. God is present in the people we let take our time because they have some need. We know the Divine in people who are our responsibility: students in our classrooms, children in the bedroom upstairs, neighbors who ask us to feed their pets while they are away. God is also present in the classes and the lesson plans we struggle over, in the creative energy expended to furnish that bedroom, in the neighbor's pet who can mirror Life and the way to live it as we watch and learn about ourselves from its behaviors.

As we become more aware and alert and alive—more contemplative—we learn to say and experience what Abraham Heschel said and knew: "Just to be is a blessing. Just to live is holy." Everything speaks of Life and touches our lives. Incarnation is radical indeed. It is so deep that it goes beneath the most deeply-rooted boundary separating spiritual from secular. As people live more and more at the heart of centered activity, without losing themselves in this process, they know what Thomas Aquinas has called the highest form of contemplation. That pinnacle of contemplative life, contemplation in action, we might call in ordinary terms living our lives with real zest.

When we are instruments of the Spirit of Jesus alive now we are contemplatives. All that is missing is a tongue of fire above each head. What these flames symbolized, however, is present: that warmth and energy of emotion that joins us to ourselves and to others. When we live as people having authority and yet bow before the Providence of God we are contemplatives. We are persons inspired as Jesus was. When we find that at the center of our own beings we meet that Being who is true Father/Mother/Nourisher, we are contemplatives. We nourish our own inner lives and enable others to nourish themselves in their lives. Depending on our enneagram space, we bring our personal dynamics into fleshing out one or another aspect of the Trinity. All together we witness to Creator, Son, and Spirit.

CHAPTER 8

The Present Moment

Everyone is called to incarnate spirituality.[1] Being human beings we can hope for nothing more. It is true that all people need to address the reality that divine and human meet in Jesus and also in themselves. Each life stance nuances this experience in a way that fits who people in that stance are, their particular instinct with its gift and compulsion, virtue and vice. Depending on which of the three basic stances is their own, people relate differently to the present where each individual reality meets the reality of the environment around it.[2]

For 2/3/4 people, those of the Spirit of Jesus alive in the world and experienced in their own spirit, the fact that humanity itself is godly becomes the important incarnational focus. For them, spiritual life is a journey within to encounter Jesus' Spirit in their self-at-home place. Other enneagram spaces may not need such an emphasis nor find anything significant in these words. But it is the godliness of humanity that resonates with 2/3/4s life issues; this realization shows them how to live the spiritual life, which means how to praise God as who they are.

That humanity is godly validates all of their living as spiritual. It directs the flow of energy inward and balances their strong outward pull. This energy outward is instinctive; it has become distorted and compulsive in the process of self-creation. Learning to live more from the inner self, just believing it exists, centers 2/3/4s and brings them into balance.

Each enneagram stance not only looks out at life differently, but each faces differing dynamics with their consequent issues in life. The compulsions of each of the three basic stances are manifested in energies that call for varying approaches to the spiritual life. These energies are expressed in images appropriate to each of them.

For 5/6/7s the image of setting forth on the journey captures their issues. Instinctive withdrawers, 5/6/7s have exaggerated this propensity into compulsion. As they move into balance and wholeness, they are called to move out to the environment and those who people it.

That Jesus, God's Son, became a human being is a growing realization in life for 5/6/7s. What does this say to them that is of particular importance on their spiritual path? Since we all learn first what is closest to our awareness, it is fitting that 5/6/7s realize their individual importance. As unique individuals they matter to the great God of the universe.

Nature images of vast expanses of sky or lofty mountain scenes touch people in this space, reminding them of their apparent insignificance contrasted with their immense value to the Creator. God who made heaven and earth is also the One who took time to see their need and respond to it by faithful and loving presence. As individuals they count in the scheme of things; God is ever mindful of them. This is what the incarnation of Jesus testifies.

Jesus has come for all people. His words and actions in scripture tell of his concern for all and his loving response to needs. Once they realize their own significance, 5/6/7s are able to follow Jesus' inspiration by offering presence to others. In this way they shape the earth in which they live together with other human beings. They learn by moving out and engaging others—a presence and an action that is as valuable to the world as perception and search for meaning. There are people who need their human touch and who offer a human touch in return. By stepping into the world around them they come to balance and move with growing comfort in creation. They have embarked on the slow and consistent journey to God in company with other travelers.

For 8/9/1s the energy issue is one of coming to hold both inner and outer worlds together. Instinctively, and later on compulsively, 8/9/1 people turn their back on one aspect of creation as they focus on the other. It is not easy for them to step away and see a continuum, a spread of awareness, from one pole of reality to the other. When they see one aspect of something, its opposite is forgotten; this opposite falls out of experience and, therefore, existence for them.

This difficulty in holding apparent opposites and contradictions occurs at the most basic level in the separation between human and divine existence. Between God and the human person a vast chasm exists. God is the all-powerful one, and creatures are powerless in the face of this majesty. How can a human being meet divinity, let alone share in that divine life? This is their question. It manifests itself in another area within their own persons: How can worldly and godly be reconciled within me? How can I ever hope to bring together the secular and spiritual aspects of myself? How can animal and angel be reconciled?

As always for the 8/9/1s the answer is not an either/or but a synthesis of these two. Humanity holds both divine and human, spiritual and secular, material and immaterial. Incarnation brings together the polarities in Jesus and in each human being whom Jesus came to save by becoming human himself and incorporating humanity into divine life. To enter fully and profoundly into human existence, neither fearing the life they share with the animals nor envying the pure vision of the angels, is the 8/9/1 call to incarnation.

The image for spiritual growth in the 8/9/1 space is one of dissolving boundaries. When there are no more divisions in their own persons or in the world around them, the lion can lie down with the lamb. There are no more wars; there is peace in the world, a world within them and around them. It becomes one world, a world of unity, but one which they must work to achieve outside by dissolving their inner punitive prejudices against parts of themselves.

The Absence of a Present Moment: The 2/3/4 Issue

Some realities that were no problem for us as small children we all need to relearn. Living in the present moment is one of these. For 2/3/4 people, the present moment does not even seem to exist:

> There really is no such thing as now. There's the past which comes up to the present. Then the future begins. The present is just the crack in between. When I look at life I see the past, then that crack, and the future all at once. Doesn't everybody do that?

The answer is no, not everybody does that. People in the 2/3/4 stance have one foot in the past and the other in the future. They tend to distort the past by exaggeration; things were either very good or very bad back there. The future is a place about which plans are made so that things can get done.

These plans are not like the dreams of the 5/6/7s; they are more concrete and usually are carried to completion. Energy in arranging for future happenings propels 2/3/4s out of the now and fixes their gaze and thinking ahead in time.

Constantly moving into the future is partly a function of their instinct toward activity of all kinds. It is, therefore, also related to anxiety. When people are anxious, they worry about all that might or might not be. One way to address this worry is to "get on top of" that future time by preparing for whatever possibilities might lie ahead. Scripts to cover various eventualities and scenarios of conversations to be used if and when this or that occurs pull 2/3/4s out of the moment. Never to be caught unprepared, never to be without a response, never to be surprised at what happens: these motivations plummet 2/3/4s into what is not yet. Even though some plans may not be used, having them provides a feeling of security.

Straddling time by coming down on the one side in memories of what was and on the other in plans for what will be, 2/3/4s need to learn that the present also has existence and dimension. Energy needs to be here and now. What makes such a focus difficult for 2/3/4s goes back to their diminished emotional function. Remember, early in life people in this stance submerged emotional experience in order to survive in the way they instinctively knew: they busied themselves; they accomplished.

Emotions give texture and dimension to life. They also slow people down to taste and savor everchanging layers of experience. There is a complete reversal of 2/3/4 instinct in tarrying over life, in taking time, as the saying goes, to smell the roses. Activity-producing anxiety denies the importance, if not the very existence, of the present. Letting in the fullness of feeling here and now affirms it.

2/3/4 people fear they have no interior life at all, or none that has the depth and quality equal to that of people in other spaces. They draw this conclusion from an awareness they are oftentimes not really "here." Their early-developed pattern of leaving the present for the past or future builds a lifetime of experience that only substantiates and increases this fear.

> I'm scared to be alone. What will I do all by myself. Is anybody home inside to spend my time with? And why would I want to anyway? Other people are what it's all about and I don't mind adapting myself for them. I enjoy going along with people. It's the only way I know how to be.

This fear of being in the present moment leads 2/3/4s to keep moving, to see as important only what propels them to outer activity and, therefore, to plunge into future planning and goal-setting. Early in the second part of life they begin to experience emotions that can no longer be successfully submerged and forgotten. Surfacing emotions often results in initial panic; this is such a new experience and something over which they have little control. As time goes on, however, the value of living from an emotional depth takes on meaning. They learn that letting in and allowing emotions joins them affectively with themselves and other people. They begin to know for themselves what is happening inside other people who are present here and now. Eventually they come to value this way of being as it becomes more familiar. Simple presence to themselves is peaceful; it is beyond loneliness. It is self—as well as other—companionship. They come to desire more of this being here and now.

Then their activity function takes over once again, but now more subtly. Of course, they cannot make emotional presence happen for themselves, though they struggle to do so. They attempt to separate themselves from this presence to critique it, an activity that immediately kills any semblance of what they are searching for. The technique they employ to become aware guarantees they will not be. Emotional waves cannot drench people who are standing at a distance watching them roll in.

Simply living is what makes the present real, and being in present reality is contemplation. Yet, there is some value for 2/3/4 people in looking at the experiences of contemplation they have had, looking back afterward to observe them. This reflective returning to the past, an activity that 2/3/4s are acquainted with, can be profitable and educational. Reflection does not come from the doing function; it is not the same as analytical work. It happens from the mental function; it is a gentle gaze, an apprehension of what was.

What needs to be remembered? The "feel" of being in the moment: sad, angry, exuberant, quiet. Although now part of the past, memory of unselfconscious, unexamined presence in that now finished experience is helpful for 2/3/4s. As they remember what being fully in the now was like, they can contrast that presence with their more frequent experiences of non-presence. They then have information out of which to distinguish and discern what it is that makes them whole. But they have no more than that. They have no information that

will insure that simply being now will happen again for them;
nor do they have the ability to re-create it.

What they do have is a memory that can help them rejoice
in the richness of their own personal interiors, their own selves,
something 2/3/4s need to celebrate. They are aware that this
present self surprised them, that there was no cause and effect
they could learn about in order to make it happen again. They
learn in still one more way that life/Life will neither let them
down nor submit to their control. They learn once again they
are creatures life/Life sweeps along in its current.

> When I have a feeling of peace I usually try to hang onto
> it. So, of course, it evaporates and I'm back to my brain
> working overtime. The only way something happens is if I
> forget about stuff and just live. Whatever that means. I'm
> not sure. It just makes me feel like I'm not doing anything
> at all and I think that's okay. In fact, it may be what life is
> all about.

Remembering has a trap, however, for 2/3/4s. It frequently
distorts reality into something other than it really was. Here the
body function can be helpful. Remembering an experience of
contemplation, 2/3/4 people might be inclined to filter out
the physical feelings that presence to self always includes. This
can lead 2/3/4s to think and to talk about what happened
when they "contemplated" as an ethereal rather than enfleshed
experience. All people tend to wall off one function from
another, and 2/3/4s are no exception to this. Accurate memory always includes the physical and prevents a heady view of
contemplation.

> I had a great summer. I caught up on some reading and
> work; went on a short trip. But it wasn't that. I just . . . well,
> my tight shoulders relaxed the whole time. That's about the
> best way I can talk about it, and that told me it was a good
> time.

If we are to become contemplative people, whatever our enneagram space, we need to be alert and awake in the present

moment. After all, we human beings are destined to live in time. Time is linear; it comes to us in a succession of discrete moments, each of which we experience as now. We have talked about how one enneagram stance finds it hard to live a contemplative existence—that is, to meet life moment-by-moment, and fully absorb it. We turn now to the issue for 5/6/7 people on the enneagram.

Compulsive Gathering of Information: The 5/6/7 Issue

Unlike 2/3/4s, 5/6/7s get stuck in the present. The one function that not only overshadows others but also becomes automatic in the present is perception. The continual bombardment of sensory stimuli, the constant adding of new information to what has already been received and organized, makes it hard for them to experience emotional and behavioral aspects of their awareness in the present.

The more 5/6/7s operate instinctively and keep collecting perceptions, the more withdrawn they become.

> My wife tells me that when I'm angry at her I get very distant. I put out all sorts of rational explanations about what we're discussing. She calls it my turning into a walking computer. I don't even notice what's happening, except that I'm feeling pretty scared about how things are going. That makes me turn to the thing I do best: keep logical and unemotional. I don't know how else to protect myself from all the feelings we're tossing back and forth.

It seems to 5/6/7s that they lack ability to function in the world. They don't know what to say or how to say it. They don't move smoothly in and out of situations, but stumble through where others seem to flow. They are so confused by all the information that keeps coming in to them that sensory overload makes them shut down and become nonfunctioning.

The detachment with which they meet others applies to their own lives, too. When they recall their past history, 5/6/7s tend to do just that and no more. They need to learn how to remember their own lives, to draw together the threads of their history, attending to each. Awareness of painful childhood experiences, significant persons, valuable choices, moving moments fill out and enrich experience. Remembering means to recall with emotion. Adding this element of feeling to the objective plot of their own lives is the self-respect 5/6/7s need to find.

There is also something about visions and possibilities for the future that 5/6/7s need to personalize and bring home to their hearts. Viewing both their past and present as interesting information and little more, they approach the future in much the same way. Options in the present turn into possibilities for tomorrow. The data from the present converts easily to considerations about uses for this data later on. Life is appraisal from the outside without action, or else it is action that does not require leaving the safe confines of the interior world.

Unconsciously at first, 5/6/7s protect themselves in the safety of perceptions. If they do not incorporate emotion with perception, they need never commit themselves to person or plan or possibility. They go on considering options and indefinitely delay dedication to any one of them. Once they realize what they have done for self-protection, they need the courage to move beyond the protective world of collecting and arranging sensory data to that place where feelings urge them out of themselves.

Only this energy of deep emotion can move 5/6/7s outside to interaction with other people, an interaction which may be either pleasant or unpleasant. When we physically contact another person, we tend to freeze in fear to the extent we are unfamiliar with allowing our bodies to relate with other bodies. Perhaps 5/6/7s experience this bodily shock more than any others. Once moved emotionally, 5/6/7s find themselves moved behaviorally. They reach out to the unfamiliar and frightening world around them with words and actions. When response comes, they recoil in shock and retreat again into the safer world of perception. The need to follow their feelings into human encounter and closeness brings them to fear, which sends them scurrying inside once more.

For this reason some people find 5/6/7s the most mystifying of people with whom to relate. After initial invitations to others, they become afraid and then lower and hide behind a curtain of perceptions. The person they both want to meet and to avoid turns once again into a safe object. From seeking encounter with another, they move again to data-gathering, which takes them back to a place of less threat. They remove themselves from the frightening world where they might be invaded. Moving out leads to that fear which necessitates another withdrawal.

One solution to this issue is to try to stay away from feelings altogether. Having no emotions assures a safe position. Just do things without emotional investment and life will be possible. But without emotion, activity is thwarted for 5/6/7s, as for us all. They become paralyzed. Doomed by whatever they choose to do, they either become immobile and lacking in human encounter or they act with no investment, so that even they do not know which of their actions holds the genuine energy only emotion can provide.

> It's very hard for me to choose to do anything at all because everything looks interesting. I'm taken by all sorts of things and enjoy considering lots of options. It's like a game. This could happen or this or that. No way do I think for a minute any of them will actually come about. I have no idea how to get from inside here to accomplishing. When I think about it I'm stymied. Only when I get really mad or grabbed by something or someone can I bridge the gap. When I find myself out there because I got carried away, I ask "Hey, how did this happen?"

The Burden of Unprocessed Emotion: The 8/9/1 Issue

For 8/9/1 persons, the present is blurred and unclear. It is a succession of disconnected moments in time. It has neither form nor shape; it is not part of any significant whole. Those who are 2/3/4s try to shape the present by ordering the outer world: who connects with whom, what roles people have, what titles fit with which persons, what response is appropriate to this environment. 5/6/7s try to fashion and order the inner world: How does this information fit with what I already know? What system gives meaning to reality? What knowledge provides the key that makes everything fall into place? But 8/9/1s see reality as unorganized, people as not connected, and one moment as having no particular relevance to another.

Since all that 8/9/1s can manage to do is cope with pieces of the present as they come along, the significance of past experience is forgotten and undigested. Situations of profound emotional significance often are unconsciously carried into and affect the present. Even though they are forgotten, these remnants of the past do not cease to be. They account for reactions and prejudgments that have an unaccountable and tenacious hold. Often, too, 8/9/1s lock in on some idea or conclusion in a way that is inexplicable to them and to others.

Sometimes there seems to be no past for 8/9/1s. They have forgotten about it. It's reality is evident, however, in apparently illogical decisions and actions in the present, which they justify by a superstructure of logic based on some affective premise that eludes them.

> My boss is a great guy, all heart and generous as they come. But sometimes he gets this fix on something and you could move heaven and earth and not convince him he's off-base. If he thinks what you're doing is for some certain reason, then it is, that's all. He knows; you just haven't realized it yet. But if you wait awhile and listen to him, you'll come to see the light—which translates into seeing things the way he does.

The future is also nonexistent. There is no point in thinking about it because one never knows what will happen. Besides, the present takes all the energy one has. Why make plans that may never come to fruition. This lack of future awareness often is noticeable in the 8/9/1 tendency toward inertia; probably more than any other space, 8/9/1s tend to continue with whatever they are about. They have difficulty picking up anchor and moving along to something new. If they are at a party, for example, they often stay until uprooted by others who are leaving. However, when a party is planned, they are often the ones unwilling to make the effort to be there.

The winds and tides of various energies demand expression, control, or banishment by denial or suppression. All of these responses call for effort and use up their resources. Unlike 2/3/4s, who push away present feelings and move to accomplishment, or 5/6/7s, who observe rather than participate in the moment, 8/9/1s are forced to grapple with the reality of their feelings somehow. They cannot ignore this instinctive emotional reaction. Efforts at managing emotions, whether these efforts are conscious or unconscious, confronting or denying, leave little energy for simply seeing and hearing. The 8/9/1 person often seems to miss the nuance of the moment, its subtlety of expression, its sensitively developed arguments. He or she needs broad, obvious strokes or repeated information so that perceptual mists can dissipate and clarity come.

Remembering, which I have defined as recall combined with emotion, serves a particular purpose for 8/9/1s as it does for the other stances. When they remember their personal experience, they digest its emotional impact more thoroughly than they were able to do back then. They discover some of the roots of the instinctive prejudgments that show up in the present, and they learn to attend to these causes. They allow the pain and discomfort and intensity of what they had previously ingested to enter a digestive process. The poisons are eliminated, nourishment absorbed, and learning utilized by their organism.

I have used the body in this image because it often helps 8/9/1s with undigested experience that is causing them present discomfort. Some bodily involvement assists their interior digestive process. Activities which prove helpful to 8/9/1s include talking issues through or expressing them in art or sculpture or mime or writing. Even the action of walking or running or striving in some sport can separate parts of their experience from the whole and help them get distance and perspective.

Once they see themselves distinct from the problem or issue or feeling or other person, 8/9/1s are able to move to objectivity. The moment seen in the perspective of time, space, and importance helps them to become aware of boundaries, proportions, and sequential elements. Activity opens avenues of perceptual clarity and assists digestion of moment-to-moment experience.

> I hate journaling. It would take me fifty pages to write down what one day is about. I never have energy to do any journaling. What I like to do is draw a picture. No content, usually. Just colors and shapes and textures that add up to the feel of what's going on with me. Words would take forever to convey what one picture does.

Once again we see the importance of image and symbol, the language of the unconscious, for 8/9/1 people. Their emotional intensity—or defensive banishing of emotional intensity—finds safe, manageable, clarifying form in a symbol, which gathers perceptions and emotions into one all-encompassing expression. Then they are able to wake up from the sleep that protected them from the distress caused when they swallowed their emotional experience whole. The image or symbol converts experience to digestible form. Then assimilation can take place.

Surprise Is a Quality of Presence

The element of surprise is always present in genuine contemplation.[3] All of us have known the feeling of simply living, of being and doing, that is unintentional, unscheduled, unplanned. We have all experienced how life leaps out in the here and now. Because there is no effort to pin it down, life takes those-who-are-present into its flow. This reality seems amazing, awesome. It is unearned; it is ordinary and yet of the utmost importance. It can be called contemplation.

We find we can do only one thing about this gift. We can celebrate and give thanks for life/Life. In so doing, we savor all that such moments have been for us, learn the dimensions of these times in the way our organisms absorbed the experience. As we do this, we grow more and more able to prefer being awake and alert in the present to using our patterned approaches to living. Gradually, as we grow in contemplation, we find ourselves growing in wisdom. This wisdom reminds us again and again that we cannot make contemplation happen; we only get in the way of its happening with our compulsions. Wisely, and by trial and error, we eventually learn how to forget efforts and live.

To put all of this still another way, we give up those efforts which ensure control over our lives. One certainty is that there will surely be an element of surprise when we are present in the moment. Life is not about yesterday's sadness or pain or intensity, today's options, tomorrow's plans. It is about presence. If any prediction is possible, it is that we will be taken by reality in ways we never would have believed possible. Nothing we would ever have made for ourselves is what we find life to be.

> If anybody would have told me thirty years ago I would be the way I am and doing what I'm doing I'd never have believed it. I'd never even have dreamed I could feel like I do about Mary and the kids and my whole life. I never planned to be who I am today, but I'm sure glad it happened.

Giving up self-creation because no self-creation brings life is the wisdom that leads to statements such as this one. It is something that could only be said later in life. Were the speaker to have analyzed each step along the way, the comment could never have been made. Somewhere along his life's path, this man learned to distinguish between the strained, self-conscious concern with maintaining his created self and the simple openness of genuine contemplation. Having so distinguished, he allowed himself to become his unique word. Now he is in awe of what life has brought him to. He has fallen to a level deeper than self-creation, to an acceptance of who he is. His plans for making himself into someone have died.

From Despair Comes Hope

The virtue of hope stands opposite that despair all people eventually experience in their efforts to make themselves who they think they ought to be. Despair is with us when we see that all the avenues of possibility and plan have been explored and all of them are dead-ended. We come to know life cannot be controlled. We cannot live in what we thought reality to be because it does not exist; it is founded on illusion and delusion. We only have now.

To have only this present feels like being trapped and enslaved, because now cannot be made more interesting or energizing or possible than it is. There is nothing to do but be here, not looking one way to all that was or the other way to all that will be. Life is truth. Scripture says what all people might do well to recall: "Now is the acceptable time; now is the day of salvation" (2 Cor 6:2). Not yesterday, not tomorrow, but now. Unadorned, present reality is where life/Life is.

Henri Nouwen writes about the hopefulness that permeated Jesus' attitude:

> Being neither an optimist nor a pessimist, Jesus speaks about hope that is not based on chances that things will get better or worse. His hope is built upon the promise that, whatever happens, God will stay with us at all times, in all places. God is the God of life.[4]

God is present now, Jesus tells us. The Way, the Truth, the Life breathes in this day and at this moment, whether we are washing the car or eating lunch or feeling that life is meaningless or enjoying the presence of someone we love. How that presence will shape our lives we cannot now know. Someday we will, however, and then we can celebrate those times when we let go of our controls and hope surprised us.

The subtlety of expectations is caught in this statement by a woman aware of her tendency to program her future.

> I don't think I have any idea how many expectations I carry around. I was planning a meeting with Bill and we were going to talk about how our relationship wasn't going well. So we decided to meet at our favorite restaurant. I had no expectations of what might happen. Like fun I didn't. I'd refused to plan how the conversation would go. I thought I was completely open, but when we got there the waitress put us at the wrong table, one in the middle of the room, not off in a quiet corner where we usually sat. I couldn't talk to him. Things weren't the way I'd planned—or not planned? So much for no expectations.

Jane and Bill did reconcile, but not at the restaurant and not the way she had anticipated. She had enough self-reflection to catch herself—and enough self-care to forgive herself—for being the way she was. She was able to let go of her instinctive, and initially unconscious, plan. When she did so she began to experience Bill himself. She listened to what he had to say and to herself and her own response to this real person. She was surprised how it happened, but it called her to continue in life with Bill, accepting both pleasant and unpleasant moments of his real presence.

For another person hope may come in the form of an invitation to enter life in a way never dreamed possible. The encouragement of another person can draw into action someone who had never dared to trust personal capabilities.

> When I began to teach I never thought I'd be anywhere but in my own classroom for the rest of my life. Then my superintendent encouraged me to go on in administration. Amazingly, I listened to what he said and began to take courses, all the time saying if it got to be too much I'd quit. Well, I finished my graduate degree and now I'm a school principal. Sometimes I wonder how this scared little kid ever got where she is now. I know it was because my

superintendent thought I could do it. Then I found out
I could.

The faith of someone else can lead to faith in oneself. This
faith is another word for self-trust and reflects the surprise of
power and strength found in human relationship. Such trust
overcomes suspicion and the fear of being victimized by others
who might take advantage of one's naivete.

For still another person, hope may take the form of satisfying
a hunger and thirst for justice. Gradually one gives one's self
over to the flow of life and moves away barriers of prejudice
that block the flow. One finds that one's individual life streams
into a great surge of unity, which replaces the trickle selfishness
and greed dam up.

> I used to sit around and whine about how unfair politics were
> in this city. What's the use, I used to say. There's nothing
> anybody can do about things. One day my precinct captain
> asked me to participate in getting information around the
> neighborhood exposing local slum landlords. I wasn't keen
> on the thing at first. It took a lot of time and effort. But
> I figured I couldn't dare complain if I hadn't tried to do
> something. I can't say we've changed the world, but now I
> know there are ways to make things happen if you're willing
> to work.

Efforts that cost time and energy and demand sacrifice can help
bring about a more just and peaceful world. The despairing
sense of being helpless in the face of overwhelming odds is
less when people work together. They come to discover that
individual efforts joined with others can make an impact. It
is no wonder that the conviction and self-sacrifice of inspired
leadership has done so much to offer hope to our world.

The Body Reveals a Hopeful Attitude

People who live in the present are flowing with life. They are
not figuring life out or planning the next step. Even their bodies
state that flow.[5] Their head relaxes above their shoulders rather

than stretches into the future. Their chin does not thrust out to meet coming challenges. Their entire organism rests rather than pulls beyond the moment and off-center. Their eyes look at what is around them, not into activities and possibilities ahead. They are available instruments for their own and others' reality.

Such people reach out spontaneously to touch and taste and smell their environment as well as to look at it. Their shoulders are not hunched over as if they expected a blow or carried a dutiful but oppressive yoke beyond their strength to bear. They do not recoil from the environment or suspect it to be hostile or frightening.

Their legs are not planted tensely in the ambivalent stance of terrified aggression. Their eyelids are not heavy and drooping as though they were napping over a heavy and undigested dose of experience. They do not nervously poke and jab with accusation and scolding, imagining the voice of the internal accuser to be outside themselves.

We might say, once again, that they are full of life/Life because they let life/Life move through them without blocking it off into mental categories or judgments about whether it is appropriate or inappropriate, right or wrong, good or bad. Besides flowing with inner life and energy, they over-flow into their incarnate bodies. Their emotions are real and immediate; their actions are confident; their insights are clear. In the deepest sense of the word they are full of life/Life and its gift, its grace. To say it in terms of the whole human organism, they are truly graceful people.

The Contemplative Attitude and Discernment

Something in us makes us want to be "on top" of our lives. From a height above our dark, hidden, mysterious, gut center, we can delude ourselves that we are gods. Mount Olympus has always been a symbol of power and divinity, of light and openness, of knowledge and rationality. People who live high up in their organisms tell themselves that they are in control of their destinies.

As human beings and creations of that Life which is our Source, we gradually learn how deceptive such thoughts can be. We learn to live from our center in the second part of our lives. That place just beneath our navel is where everything above and below meet in balance. No human being stays in this place all the time, simply because nobody is flawless. However, it is also probably true that by the time we reach adulthood we have experienced a feeling of centeredness at least for passing moments.[1]

Such times always involve bodily relaxation, which accompanies an interior attitude of letting go; we allow walls and barriers to dissolve and ourselves to be taken into the flow of life. The efforts of trying to achieve centeredness will never bring it about, however. When our organism is ready, when it has lived with its compulsions long enough, this relaxation happens.

When we relax into life, we find energy that draws downward to center, to gut. By going with that energy we give up the need to have the future clarified and assured. We abandon ourselves to that primitive wisdom which says that life is found by an allowing stance rather than by one which grasps at control. In the bowel area, where power to conceive and nurture life resides, we are often mystified and sometimes frightened by our own primitive, irrational responses. In compulsion we pull up and away from these strong urges the present moment hold us to. Gradually we realize we must admit these urges, acknowledge their undeniable existence. We learn how restful, calm, and strong it can feel to live from such honesty in our bodies. The more often we touch this kinesthetic experience, this body feel, the more we are willing to endure the recurring fears when we find ourselves falling into and being carried along by life's current.

Everyone knows the feeling of pulling away from this center, blocking off its primitive, downward pull and straining up toward control. For all spaces, relaxation means centered, gut living. And yet everyone has learned the pattern of compulsive denial of this place of balance. Depending on our enneagram space we move out of our centered energy to that body area where we are most instinctively comfortable and at home. For 2/3/4s, off-center living means tension located in shoulders and chest where plans for achievement push toward the future and deny the present. For 5/6/7s, energy moves up to the head where more and more information seems to assure a control over life and replaces the frightening abandonment to wherever life might lead. For 8/9/1s, the place of tension is the heart, where judgments of like or dislike are so instinctive and, therefore, familiar.

The message of the body (strain, pain, nausea, relaxation), the message of emotion (fear, sadness, joy, anxiety), the message of perception (insight, perceptual connection, assessment, decision), make up the inclusive approach that involves all of our functions. This is the contemplative attitude we need to recover if we are to remove those boundaries we established early in our lives and engage more and more in the second task of our lives. Gradually we include functions we had buried and of which we are now aware.

> I never knew anger until I was about 35. Somewhere around that time I began to notice I'd get very busy sometimes. I'd clean house or work in the garden or catch up on all sorts of little jobs around the house. I began to realize I did those things when I wanted to register some complaint against my husband or kids. I was saying, "I'm angry at you." I think they already had learned to read it that way, but I hadn't said it to myself until that day when I became aware.

Our organism has written emotion and action in its own language of energy. We owe a great deal to bioenergetic therapists who teach us we cannot lose sight of ourselves as enfleshed, that we respond to everything inside and outside ourselves as complete organisms, all of one piece, incarnate.

Perhaps their most valuable learning from the point of view of human growth is the inseparable link between our energies, our emotional life, and our clear perception of reality. We human beings have access to the flow of our lives to the degree that we allow our energies to speak to us. Although we do not have to give expression to everything of which we become aware, we must admit at least to ourselves whatever we feel or judge. If we cut ourselves off from our activity or our emotional or perceptual functions, we deny ourselves the energy we need to live.[2]

What bioenergetic therapists are saying, of course, is what we have discussed in earlier chapters. Early in life we judge certain emotional responses, opinions, ideas, and physical sensations unacceptable because they do not fit our image of how to survive in the world of adults. We soon forget these aspects even exist. To remember and experience them is to cause ourselves conflict. Better not to be angry at all when to do so means we talk back to our parents, act resentful, refuse to cooperate,

and know the unpleasant results of having done these things.
Keep fear hidden; if people know we are afraid they will scold
or make fun of us. Keep silent so as not to be punished for
over-exuberance. Never admit you are in pain because people
will call you a baby. Don't act spontaneously or they will see
too much of who you are.

Judgments about part of our experience lead to denial or
to inhibited behaviors, which eventually cause us to forget we
feel the way we do, think the way we do, behave the way
we do. We all create boundaries of judgment that block off
parts of our reality. We all, therefore, cut ourselves off from
sources of energy. We all need to open ourselves to more and
more of our denied and forgotten experience. Only when we
listen to clues concerning blocked energies can we live fully
human, conscious, and awake. In knowing our truth, we can
then choose what of it to express outside and what to retain as
our own private experience.

> Every night before I go to sleep I ask myself, as I'd ask any
> good friend, what her day has been like. So much of my life
> is taken up with distractions from inside and out that I'm
> often completely unaware of how things are going for me.
> Reminding myself I'm my friend helps too.

Although boundary-making and denying as it applies to loss
of energy are common to everybody, they have application for
each basic stance that is unique. Like everything else that is part
of being human, the dynamic of living complete lives is nuanced
according to our enneagram space. We view our emotional
lives, our lives of activity, and our perceptual awarenesses differently depending on which function is primary, which most
deeply buried, which helpful as a bridge between the two.

> When I get a sore throat it usually means I'm sad about
> something but I can't admit it. At some point while I'm
> doctoring myself with gargles and cough syrup or whatever,
> I usually realize this and I let the tears come out my eyes and
> nose. I even let myself cry aloud if I'm alone. Then my sore

> throat goes away. Now that I know how it works, when I
> begin getting the sore throat I start out with the question,
> "What am I sad about that I don't want to admit?"

The way by which we come to know God, a God who lives where all of our reality is owned and allowed existence, is what some spiritual masters call active contemplation. Another way to say this is that we do what we can do to prepare, to be ready and waiting with all of who we are for union with the word/Word of self/Self. We let ourselves be aware of our total human experience, inside and outside us, moment to moment. And again, if our spiritual life does not involve our complete organism, if we hold off our energy in perception, activity, or feeling instead of knowing all three, we cannot fall past these functions and these centers in our upper bodies to our gut, home of the self and place of balance.

The gift of self-dwelling, of God-dwelling, called passive contemplation follows our active awareness and alert consciousness of our self-created boundaries. We learn those places where in early life we sealed off energies. Letting go is a gift that comes when we least expect it and beyond any cause and effect of efforts and their consequences. It is life's/Life's gift pulling us into the flow; hence, we call it passive.

> I spent most of my life swallowing what was going on with
> me. I saved my tears for when I got to bed, or hit my pil-
> low and swore late at night instead of when I felt like it. I
> couldn't get back what I'd put on hold, though. It was gone.
> I was gone. I'd done such a good job denying my own reality
> that I'd completely lost myself and I couldn't get me back. It
> feels great just to find something inside me giving up the old
> ways once in awhile. It makes me feel close to me. Close to
> God, too.

The journey to this center where my word is expressed and where I find God's Word, does not detour around emotions or perceptions or behaviors. Our entire self, no longer denied in mental or body or affective functioning, eventually and increasingly lets go to the pivotal balance point of quiet gut living. Here the hidden world of the-whole-of-who-I-am has always existed, waiting to be recognized.

Anthony de Mello makes this simple awareness clear in his stories about the master who again and again describes for his disciples that ego-less state beyond self-awareness, self-reflection, self-assessment.

> "There are three stages in one's spiritual development," said the Master. "The carnal, the spiritual, and the divine."
>
> "What is the carnal stage?" asked the eager disciples.
>
> "That's the stage when trees are seen as trees and mountains as mountains."
>
> "And the spiritual?"
>
> "That's when one looks more deeply into things—then trees are no longer trees and mountains no longer mountains."
>
> "And the divine?"
>
> "Ah, that's Enlightenment," said the Master with a chuckle, "when trees become trees again and mountains, mountains."[3]

From mindlessness to mindfulness and beyond to simply living life, being contemplative, is another way to talk about life's two tasks. De Mello says through the mouth of the Spiritual Master who tells his stories that we move from observing what is around us to being aware of the deeper meaning of all that exists, and then we move to that final stage of enlightenment or fullness of living where we again just live life.

Until we can trust both our inner and outer life, we cannot let go of control and trust the self. It is the self that "inhabits" that center beneath the navel in the bowel area. The self is individual life energy. We learn in life to fall out of our heads, beneath our body skeletons, past the soft organs of our torsos—primarily our hearts—into personal life energy, the self in the gut center.

Presence to personal life energy joins the individual to Life itself, the Divine, nearer to us than we are to ourselves and discovered when we are with our selves. Once we are in this center we no longer need to reflect on one or another human function: mental, affective, or bodily.

What Discernment Means

At this point I would like to link what I have described here to what spiritual writers call discernment. Sometimes genuine discernment is wrongly seen as a mental decision about what is good followed by an act of will to carry out that good. I would say, rather, that discernment is the awareness of centered or not-centered energy in the organism.[4]

This awareness comes from an accumulated awareness of who we fully and genuinely are. It is knowing where our center—and hence our life—resides, as well as where it does not. It assumes experience has revealed how and where we flee in efforts to control life, to be our own god. It unmasks those dynamics by which we exaggerated perception or feeling or activity because they were instinctive to us. Discernment also lays open the parts we had to bury to maintain this false picture of ourselves.

As life builds up more and more sense of our total selves, more and more inclusion of body, mind, and emotion in our self-experience, it becomes less and less possible for us to choose against ourselves. We become less influenced by the fear that caused us to resist growing and developing into the persons we were meant to be. We come to accept ourselves and to know the Divine experientially, and this experience invites us again and again into life/Life. Discernment necessitates a decision to flow with life or to resist it. We can either pull away from our true center and up to that exaggerated center we have used as a basis for defining who we think we ought to be, or else we can relax trustingly and let life lead. The choice is ours.

But life becomes increasingly irresistible. It becomes harder and harder in the second part of our lives to violate our own selves, our very word, because we have learned how self-violation feels and how self-regard and self-dignity are preferable to it. When we learn to discern our genuine experience of being off-center and on-center, we grow increasingly aware of what it means to live. Once one has "seen God," the scriptures say, one finds God nearly impossible to resist. Life, "godliness," is so desirable that it takes immense energy to hold it off.

Discernment well-made—that is, experience well-known—makes choice natural, even easy. Choice is that decision either to retain boundaries of judgment manifested by blocked body energies or to risk letting in everything we are. When we can accept what we previously denied, we move beyond the fear of dying and into the dark and mysterious experience of living. In doing so we abandon predictions of how life will turn out, judgments of what is good or bad, assessments of what does or doesn't fit. We simply live from our center.

Now becomes the acceptable time, the day of salvation. We learn to live there more and more, not because it is law or rule or duty to grow in awareness, to have a more contemplative attitude, but because it gives us a sense of wholeness and centeredness, of living from the self. At this place of self, our true center of balance, we find our life/Life.

God is no longer in our past experience, helpful as it may have been along the way to remember life there. Nor is God in our plans and visions for the future, because there is nothing of future life we can predict, let alone experience. We are only creatures in time who meet reality moment by moment. We only have the poverty and emptiness—and fullness as well—of the present.

Our entire organism feels content with what is, like a weaned child is content, as the psalmist says, on its mother's lap (Ps 131). We live as relaxed as that child, and we are nourished by the Divine Mother at the center of who we are, body and spirit, incarnate being, human organism.

Contemplative Awarenesses and Discernment in the Nine Points

Initially this book discussed the first task of life, which is common for everyone. It went on to speak of how this task takes shape for those who look out at life from each of the three basic stances. Now we will speak of how each stance within the three basic ones nuances the dynamics of the stance they share. We will look at that particular compulsion in each of the three numbers and consider dynamics that perpetuate the lies of childhood and frustrate the unique contribution of that point to the whole human creation. Hopefully, such a discussion will specify our individual call still further and make discernment as it has been described more informed.

Before we begin to discuss each of the nine numbers, I would like to comment on a pattern that applies to each of the three basic stances.[5] The first number in each of these stances affords an obvious statement of that stance's dynamics. For example, 2s express outwardly the movement toward others, the importance of connecting, finding value in what one does, and the other traits we have discussed as applying to 2/3/4s. The 5s obviously enflesh traits of the 5/6/7s: withdrawal, hyper-perceptivity, a feeling of being of no account to others, and further characteristics outlined for 5/6/7s. The 8s express the dynamics of 8/9/1s, including ground-holding, an exaggerated feeling function, the importance of power, and other aspects discussed in relationship with 8/9/1s. It is as though 2s, 5s, and 8s see and accept their characteristics more easily than the other numbers in their stance. They not only are more comfortable with these traits, they experience their own dynamics positively. "Is there any other way to live life?" is the attitude they manifest.

Persons in the middle number—or shock point—of each stance are so deeply permeated with it that they find it difficult even to perceive that dynamic. The compulsions, the issues for growth, the resistances of 3s, 6s, and 9s blind them. They find it harder to separate from their issues in order to assess their situations consciously and know who they are and who they need to become.

The last numbers in each space do possess the dynamics of that stance, but they do not like the way they know themselves to be. The 4s, 7s, and 1s experience what feels like a double response. The first energy pulls them toward their characteristic instinct; the second, which follows immediately upon the first, urges them to express something very different from what they instinctively would manifest. Thus, 4s respond initially as 2/3/4s would, but, because this is not something seen as a desirable way to be, present a more aloof attitude. As someone in this space once said: "I cling, but only on the inside." The 7s, who recoil in fear, judge this to be undesirable and so immediately modify the response to outgoing friendliness. Their terrified eyes above smiling lips often give away this double dynamic. The 1s, who instinctively outline their territory and are self-preserving, see this as a selfish and bad way to be, and so they move out in kindly service and caring attention. They, as do 4s and 7s, lack the genuine expression of people who respond instinctively from their true dynamic. Instead, they consciously choose another dynamic to replace their own.

With these descriptions as a prelude, and holding them in mind, we look at the nine numbers in turn to see how each space grows in contemplative awareness and learns to let go and fall into life's stream. This process of denying and then relaxing into the reality life later reveals is summed up in enneagram theory in the consideration of vices and virtues. We describe briefly our early deceptions and later awarenesses as these apply specifically to each of the nine enneagram numbers or points.[6]

Pride/Humility

For 2s, who genuinely believe that only activity gives them worth, the issue is to face the fear that underlies activity. What will happen to them if they stop helping other people? Once the outer covering of taking care of others and their needs is peeled off, does anything remain? The terror of finding nothing left, of standing on the brink of an inner world that doesn't exist, keeps 2s outside themselves. It is this terror they must face and acknowledge before conversion can happen.

> When I sit in my chair quietly and try to turn inside to myself, I find myself looking into absolutely nothing. I'm empty. A huge void. Nobody's home, as they say. Secretly, I think I've always considered myself a spiritual airhead. All I'm good for is filling needs.

This experience of limitation and poverty, of no bountiful interior storeroom from which to dispense the largess of service and kindness, is what leads 2s to a place of honesty, of humility. Once they admit their own needs, their personal lack cries out from their emptiness for satisfaction. They discover that the way they have ministered to others in need must become the model for ministering to self. They abandon the pretense of endless giving that denies any necessity for replenishment. Relationships, which once carried only the dimension of helper/helpee, become genuinely mutual ones.

> I'm learning to say things like, "No, I can't do that for you." On the one hand that feels right, but it blows my image of what I want people to think about me, and, frankly, what I want to think about myself. Then I remind myself I wasn't born to be the Messiah, and I laugh and get some perspective on what I've been doing because of how I've seen myself all my life. Playing God, that is. People say they like my clay feet. They don't feel so guilty for not being able to do the impossible things I seem to be able to get done.

Deceit / Truth

For 3s, who are perhaps more invested in presenting what they consider a favorable self-image than any other space, conversion involves taking time from activity to stop and look at deceptions: where, why, and how have they created someone who must always appear capable, successful, and positive. The best response in every situation, the perfect way of handling whatever comes up in life, the need to be the one who knows and does best, the necessity to place all blame for whatever goes wrong on others who got in the way of projects and plans, crescendos throughout life's first task for 3s. Eventually they so live a lie that they dare not look back to the past or into their experience for fear of some truth they may uncover. They instinctively lie or exaggerate to assure this image of themselves. While they no longer know what it was that led them to run so far and so hard from their reality, by adulthood they are certain it must have been something monstrous.

> I don't know what I expect to find when I look inside, but I'm sure it's awful. What I don't know won't hurt me, so I want to forget this interior work stuff. I don't know how to do it anyway. Just get on with life and no postmortems on anything. They will only depress me.

What 3s come to learn is how to admit the truth of who they are and the deceptions they have used to cover it over. The fear that led them to hide their own inadequacies, incompetencies, and failures needs to be faced. They must acknowledge that life exists for them only in honestly allowing instead of manufacturing themselves. As one 3 has put it, "I am what I am no matter what I do." Someone else has said it this way:

> I've spent my whole life trying to be the perfect son, student, then doctor, husband, and father. I'm 40 years old and I'm tired of all those efforts to cover up everything that wouldn't contribute to that picture. I'm actually at the point where I'm so worn out all I can do is let it all hang out—the good stuff and the bad. I don't even care anymore.

Envy/Equanimity

For 4s, the issue is one of contentment with things as they are. Fear of finding the present too ordinary leads 4s to manufacture significance and then inject it into the present. Situations causing anguish or ecstasy are preferable to pedestrian days spent in pedestrian endeavors. What is so frightening about simple living for 4s? Perhaps there may not be enough in the everyday to keep them alive. Reality may become so humdrum that they will lose energy for that intense search for meaning they feel they need to qualify as persons.

> Sometimes I wonder why I'm always figuring out myself and my relationships and the people in my life. Friends are always after me to lighten up. They ask me why I have to pick away at myself and everybody else instead of relaxing and enjoying things. For me it always has to be some self-confrontation or else analyzing motivations in me or in other people. If I don't do that I feel guilty somehow. I guess I feel I'm not taking the task of being a person as seriously as I ought to. Then I look at others who seem so genuine and approachable and present. Being human looks so effortless for them. For me it's constant scrutiny.

Shaping and honing life is the instinctive task for 4s. Experientially, they discover that what they try to make beautiful and romantic—the reality of the present moment— remains always half-formed and unfinished. The story of life keeps going on beyond their feeling of being totally inept, irrevocably abandoned, forever unredeemable, completely untranslatable. Life unfolds and changes; there are beginnings and endings which remind them of birth and death. They alternately imitate children's forgetful whimsy or brood over life's contradictions, being sometimes willing and at other times unwilling to join the human race. The price of being human is to forget about making life into polished significance and to be content with it moment by moment.

> Probably my best times are when I'm not even wondering about whether they're good or bad—or anything at all. I had everybody over for the holidays. I didn't expect much. It was just another Thanksgiving. No picture of myself as the perfect hostess. No plan of how I wanted to present myself either to me or to the group. It was just a plain old Thanksgiving. I cooked. I had a good time. Not a great time, just a good one. I don't often have just plain good times.

Avarice/Detachment

For 5s, the question of offering others what 5s possess is both problem and necessity. The deep feelings, the carefully pondered insights, the significant expressions that enrich their imaginings are meant for a broader world than the one inside themselves. It may not occur to them that they not only have gifts from within, but their very selves to share. Their world is one in which others can participate. Their own riches can be multiplied in the back and forth of human exchange. Rather than keep to themselves what they think they might need, they have to learn to give it away, trusting that when they lack for knowledge or experience or even concrete necessities, these will somehow come if they are in relationship and communication with others.

> I'm not doing the work for that group anymore. Nobody does a thing but me to get ready for our meetings and I end up spending all the effort and they get the credit. Not anymore. If they want something to happen they're going to have to do it themselves. I'm tired of being used and then not acknowledged.

Genuine detachment for 5s, in contrast to the disengagement which is their compulsion, allows them to hold their possessions—whether these be in the world of perception or of the concrete—lightly and freely. They need to see themselves as stewards of knowledge and possessions who put out what is theirs, rather than misers who pile up what they might some-day need for protection. With such an attitude, they can open their hands and let go of what is their own, what they have fostered and tended and worked through and figured out. Even more, they can entrust themselves to others they know will respect them.

> I never used to believe anybody was interested in me. I've learned, though, that I not only have something to offer, but that it is respected. No, I've learned I'm respected. I matter to people. Jane taught me that first. Now I can see it's true for other people, too.

Fear/Courage

For 6s, the issue is to address the constant ambivalence between moving into relationship with people and situations in spontaneous response or withdrawing to a safe world away from threat. They put out invitations for engagement which, when accepted, lead them to wonder about having been so bold. Additional information about others or changes in situations lead them to reconsider what they initially had assessed and acted on. Perhaps, they think, more time and care should have preceded moving out. Had they known at first what time and experience later revealed, they might have withheld engagement. The price, the consequences, the sufferings that result from risking involvement in life often lead to withdrawing early promises of fidelity to people and circumstances.

> When everybody's excited about going some place together I get all caught up in the planning. It sounds great, and I have all sorts of ideas about what we can do. But I usually back out before we actually leave. I think of all sorts of reasons why not to go along. I get scared of both what won't get done at home and what might happen while we're gone. Some of my friends get pretty put out about it, but I can't help that.

The need to follow through, to be faithful to what one has promised even at the cost of safety and the price of suffering, takes courage for 6s. They deny consistent response to others as they do to themselves. Moving little-by-little and predictably costs them much energy. Should they offer fidelity when new information might show the foolhardiness of doing so? Waiting might provide just the information that would clarify whether investment would be wise. Yet if they wait for absolute security, they will never venture forth. Having decided for and begun to risk, they need the courage to continue along the way they have begun to go, letting each day reveal the cost of their decision and action.

> It's very hard for me to stay in relationship with Pat. I find
> myself sitting back and assessing every word she says and
> everything she does as though I were involved in writing
> one of my articles instead of in my marriage. I have to stop
> myself and realize we're in this together and unless I let her
> know where I am and we both work on things together,
> we're done for. Pat knows all this already, of course. I'm the
> one who has to have the reminders.

Gluttony / Sobriety

For 7s, fear is at the base of the dynamics they find along
the path of becoming their true word. Intense tactile, auditory,
visual, and kinesthetic sensations serve to increase imaginings
of what pain, deprivation, and suffering must be like. Fanta-
sized terrors lead them to distract themselves with what speaks
to them of the good life, the safe life, the life of encouraging and uplifting possibilities. If they can hide themselves from
frightening hardship and tasteless and barren days in happier
perceptions, they believe they will have enough intellectual or
physical satisfaction to survive the present.

> There are times I feel like I'm about 5 years old. I want
> something and I want it now. It might be a partner, because
> I'm lonely and I can't stand to be lonely. Or it might be some
> book that promises to show me some incredible information
> I've been searching for. Whatever it is, I want it yesterday.
> And I'm going to get it, you can be sure of that.

The childish defense of whistling in the dark, pretending
they are unafraid, leads 7s to present an appearance of being
cheerful and happy. Underneath this image lies the perpetual
shadow of a reality where pain and suffering are entwined with
joy and pleasure. Reality as mature persons perceive and face
it shines through the pretense about life as always interesting
and enjoyable. Facts about life are often sobering. They call
for suspended fulfillment, difficult confrontation within oneself and in relationship, mundane and repetitive activity. They
need to acknowledge, embrace, and comfort their inner child,

who is frightened of the real world and desirous of making it kinder and easier. Admitting their fear and accepting it helps them look more calmly and honestly into the face of reality as it exists. They can then incorporate genuine pain and suffering into their experience and absorb people and situations as they are.

> I'm so full of my job and its many facets and my friends and all we do together, that I hate to go home to my crummy little apartment. I almost never get there until I'm ready to fall into bed and so exhausted I don't even have to look at the place. It's so small and I feel so cold and empty when I get inside. Every time I go through the door it makes me shiver. So I stay away from there as much as I can.

Lust/Innocence

For 8s, there is a constant struggle between integrity, which allows them to express interior passion, and the defense of hiding intense fear or grief or love or pain. To reveal where they can "be gotten" is to give up their best defense against being controlled by others. Passions that show and are not kept bottled up inside can no longer engulf them. Neither can they perpetuate the image of invincible power. The very act of letting out feelings that tend to build up and blind them relieves pressure, clears perception, and re-establishes self-mastery for 8s. But it also lets others see where they are invested and, consequently, where they can be wounded or deprived.

> I was so mad at myself the other day. I blew my cool and let one of my colleagues see how much that new project means to me. I'll bet now he'll use that against me. He can threaten me with dropping it whenever we're down to the wire on something. Damn, I wish I hadn't done that. But it's too late now. I'll just have to be on my guard. Probably, if I pretend I'm not interested in it anymore, I can fool him.

Protectively hiding spontaneous feeling is an instinctive denial of the interior child whose trusting response has been taken advantage of. It is this dynamic that 8s need to let go of in the second part of life. Choosing again the openness that allows interaction brings 8s beyond issues of power and weakness. They stop pushing down emotions and grow to self-mastery and self-entrusting. The pressure of pent-up feelings, which can overwhelm them if refused expression, relaxes to a trusting exchange. Honest emotion enables them to be in charge of themselves even as they risk others' taking advantage of this truth. The image of warfare is replaced by one of peaceful exchange.

> There's something about me that's very gentle. I need to protect that place and I do, except where my family is concerned. I never hide how much they mean to me. I let them see me cry when I'm moved, if you can believe that. When my kid got a scholarship last year the tears rolled down my cheeks all the way home. Somehow, with them I don't worry they'll use it against me. But what the heck, even if I did, it'd be too late. I've let them see it all.

Sloth / Action

For 9s, the more shut down and bored they become, the more sure they can be that emotions are trying to rise to the surface. Instinctively they deny the very existence of feelings, which are perhaps more strongly felt here at the shock point of the emotional center than anywhere else on the enneagram. Consequently they experience and express very little feeling. This denial of emotion provides a sense of inner control as well as an outer power, which is effective even though it is passive. It is a power manifested in lack of response rather than response.

> When my wife wants me to show her some sign of affection I don't. No emotion on demand for me. The more she asks, the less I want to do it. I just pick up the paper and begin to read and usually she goes away. If she does persist: "Do you love me?" I'll yawn and say "I love you" with about as little enthusiasm as I can muster. Sort of like, "Okay, if you insist, baby, I'll say the words."

As life goes on for 9s they begin to realize how pushing down emotional response has protected them from intensity of feeling and its consequence. They learn to acknowledge their fear of being overwhelmed and eventually to accept their experience of powerful affective energy. They become less stuck. Their admitted feelings begin to flow through them and outside them. They experience the energy of emotion as it breaks through their habitual inertia. Their eyes light up, they can decide and act, they move in life as more alert and responsible people.

> I haven't been able to do anything at the office since my divorce. I can hardly get up in the morning, let alone get any work done. I started therapy recently, and I'm just beginning to get in touch with how furious I am at that man. Even more, I'm sad about all that's happened between us. Just the other day I threw the pots and pans around the kitchen and then sat down on the floor and sobbed for about an hour. Just sobbed. Then I went to work and wrote up a report that was due a month ago.

Resentment/Serenity

For 1s, who are driven by a merciless inner judge, the issue is one of turning and facing this powerful accuser as the limited and fallible persons they are. Giving up and giving in to unending insistence on perfection is both to be defeated by and to defeat this judge. People who are 1s need to recognize that what they see as others' demands are really those of an interior self-accuser. When they can accept their human limitations they find peace. Rebellion over unanswerable demands yields to a quiet admission of imperfection. Screaming insistent inner accusations about weakness and human frailty no longer meets with attempts to prove these accusations false. Giving up infallibility is the only strategy that ends the battle.

> I've always felt guilty about my job, maybe because I'm self-employed and do pretty much the things I like to do and know I can do. But I feel I need to justify every move I

make. I keep thinking about all those people who hate their jobs and I wonder why I'm so lucky. Of course, I work my tail off. I'm my own boss so I do all the dirty work as well as the part I like. But that's never the part I think about. In some ways I might even be happier doing something I hated. At least then I'd think I was getting what I deserved and not feel I was pampering myself—which I'm not, but which I keep telling myself I am.

1s need to realize and accept that they are the people making demands of themselves. Neither the environment nor people in it are asking for more than they can give. They see their desire for rebellion as not allowable, so it is not allowed; their anger never becomes enkindled to passion, but is dampened by guilt to subtle, smoldering resentment. They need to learn that there is no enemy out there to fight against. No truce is needed because war was never declared except on the inner battlefield where they fight against the inner judge.

I've been in justice causes most of my life. I remember protests I was involved in when I was younger and the fury I had because others wouldn't respond the way I thought they should. I'm not sure who I was angrier at, those I was protesting against or those I was protesting with but who weren't as motivated as I was. After a while I realized I was most furious at myself for not being able to meet all the problems of society. I'm still as involved as ever, but I'm more effective. I'm less disappointed with people. Not me, not anybody. Maybe that's the way to a peaceful world.

Summary Remarks for the Nine Spaces

Other dynamics influence people in the various enneagram spaces. Even the dynamics mentioned here have varying nuances for individuals; the struggle between vice and virtue may take on forms other than the summary here suggests. And yet, something of the interplay between the vices or compulsions and virtues or redeeming movements described here for each space will be recognizable, however nuanced in specific cases.

Realization of these themes has led enneagram theorists to assign a vice and virtue to each space. There is wisdom in the use of such terms. Each space encounters a blindness from which those who inhabit it need to be saved; each space also provides a particular form of clear vision.

Becoming contemplative allows authentic experience to surface for 2/3/4s, truthful experience for 5/6/7s, and integrity of experience for 8/9/1s. From the lies and deceptions we come to recognize as defenses in ourselves, we learn how life has pulled off the scales from our eyes as it pulled away those of St. Paul. We become more able to look into the depths of both our loneliness and our need to incorporate ourselves into human community.

Admitting our need, we can admit a forgiving Savior. Seeing our self-victimization, we can become merciful toward ourselves. Once aware and awake, we can return home, journey out, surrender ourselves. However we need to do it, we come to balance and unity. Boundaries fall away. We are made whole, inside and out.

CHAPTER 10

The Way to Contemplation

All of life is intended to be prayer. The purpose of human existence is to live in awareness of our creatureliness as this relates to a Creator, because this is our reality. St. Paul tells us we are to do all for God's glory, even eating and sleeping. St. Thomas Aquinas calls this human endeavor, for which we are all intended, a life of contemplation in action.

How to move from our isolated desert interior with the do's and don'ts that prevent our entering into life's energetic flow is the question we all must answer. Who our true self is and how we live freely from that word becomes more and more the concern in life's second phase. Spiritual life becomes increasingly synonymous with life, personal and individual life with Life itself. The Divine infuses and transforms us when we move out of the way and give up the need to call ourselves god. We find ourselves entering into an ever greater sense of community. This is a belonging, first of all, with aspects of who we find ourselves to be. We are also more united with other people who are, like we are, imperfect yet lovable. We grow in union with a God we now know as faithfully loving.

We come to this place of community and belonging out of our isolation and loneliness. We are no longer alienated because we have grown in an attitude of contemplation. We grow in this attitude because we have had courage to open our eyes and see what we once thought was too frightening to look at. We let reality touch our total organism: thoughts, ideas, insights, emotions, feelings, body experiences of all kinds.

Sometimes we do this in an informal way, while we are riding the bus or making dinner or working on the computer or teaching a class. Other times we more formally and specifically turn to the task of seeing and hearing and connecting our perceptions of the inner and outer worlds and honoring our emotions.

We often call those more structured times our periods of prayer. Prayer is not limited to such times, as we all know well. Who cannot remember moments set aside to "pray" when nothing happened? Perhaps we fell asleep or began to daydream or became so wrapped up in self-observation that the time seemed fruitless. Most of us can also remember moments when, out of nowhere, we knew an immediacy of experience of self or other or the Divine. Often these moments were unlikely ones. We never can predict encounters with life, whether our own, other people's, or God's. Passive contemplation is the gift of the presence of life in us, the presence of the life of another, the presence of Divine Life. It is called passive because it is not consequent to our efforts; we cannot make it happen. Neither is it a reward for good behavior.

Active contemplation, on the other hand, is what we do to be awake and ready to receive. If we come from a formal religious background, we probably learned how to be awake to reality by taking time for prayer. Most religious people go through a phase in which they consider prayer fruitful when they carry on a dialogue in their imagination with their current projection of who God is. They define prayer at this period in life as conversation with God. They say that they do not pray if they neglect or are unable to fantasize such dialogue.

Later on in life prayer takes on a broader dimension, becoming contemplative, what we call the second task of life. By definition this is a spiritual task. In this form of prayer we learn receptivity by trial and error. We have no guarantee that those moments we choose to spend in prayer will be filled with presence and encounter, but we take time anyway, especially early in life's second phase. Later on, when our interior barriers are fewer and our life flows increasingly into a whole, we may not need to take times to pray as often or as long as we did when we were learning to be contemplative, waking up to reality.

Some people commenting on spiritual helps refer to times of prayer; others are less specific about formal prayer and take in multiple aspects of living that assist personal authenticity, honesty, and integrity. Aids to growth in contemplation differ for people depending on their outlook on life, instincts, and compulsions. What might be helpful to one person could feed the compulsion of another. What fits one person's life flow might have little meaning for someone else with a different dynamic.

As we might expect, the enneagram applies not only to what we need to see and hear and attend to in life, but also to the way we arrive at that seeing, hearing, and attending. All of life is spiritual experience, because all we consider as being alive takes place in oneness with the Source of who we are.

We have spoken already of the surprises that come to people as life goes on for them. And yet what is surprising for one space is very evident for another. Passive contemplation sheds light into our shadows, which were formed out of what we had to exaggerate and deny. Now we speak about active contemplation, which is the specific way to readiness for that gift of light and life we need, depending on who we innately are.

Still Moving: Helps Toward Contemplation for 2/3/4s

The spirituality of 2/3/4s is a horizontal one. There is no inclination to look toward the heavens to find the Divine. One only need turn to one's own heart and the hearts of others to find life/Life and spirit/Spirit. The spirit/Spirit is alive in the world because the community of faithful disciples is alive. They enflesh this Spirit in their own flesh as they gather in Jesus' name.

Coming together for common prayer is an experienced need for all people because we all have a social dimension. For those in the 2/3/4 stance this social instinct is of special significance. The assembly itself makes a statement that Jesus has not left humanity orphaned. His Spirit accompanies them in this time, and they have a strong need to say that together as believers. Remember, people are what life is about for them. Liturgical and shared prayer celebrates and symbolizes in the very gathering of spirits that God's Spirit is present.

It may well be that no particular fervor results from praying in a group for 2/3/4s. Distractions are present, many of them about future projects or about concerns affecting the people with or for whom they are praying. The quality of relationship with those people is also likely to fill their thoughts. And yet, to come together is no mere ritual. It is an interior necessity flowing from their strong social instinct. Prayer in common is an urgent need, even though it is oftentimes fraught with seemingly irrelevant considerations.

For 2/3/4s, the question of interiority, of presence to the self/Self is pivotal. Touching emotion and allowing it to permeate the moment with its energy is life's most difficult task. Persons in this space are not frightened by emotion in the same way 8/9/1s may be. They do not fear being overwhelmed, drowned by their feelings. They do tend, however, not to want to get into feelings, because to do so might make them nonproductive, nonfunctional. It can be true that the amount of external and pragmatic product often is less when 2/3/4s allow their emotions, with their consequent energies, to surface. Presence is heightened and priorities changed for 2/3/4s. Being with and for self and others takes precedence over compulsively doing in order to prove themselves adequate.

When 2/3/4s begin to hear about centering prayer, they tend to translate descriptions of it into a quieting down that approaches somnolence and is one expression of what spiritual writers call quietism. The kind of interior silence that 2/3/4s need to find is not a bored sleepiness, an inner blankness, a turning off of consciousness. When centered, 2/3/4s are awake and alert, filled with an influx of emotions, which they tend to judge as either positive or negative. But these emotions make them aware of themselves in a new way and invite them to a new experience of energy. These genuine emotions and the energy that being "in touch" makes possible attract them to their interior because they feel enlivening.

Truly centered persons, 2/3/4s come to discover as they grow in contemplation, are not quieted down but alive and washed with emotion after emotion. They let themselves be taken by the feelings of each successive moment. Sometimes, to their chagrin, 2/3/4s realize they must sacrifice efficiency and adaptability for authenticity. They become people for whom interior darkness is no longer an expectation or an ideal. They come to recognize that life/Life inside and outside fills them with energy and is the fruit of centering. Where they once anticipated finding a desert of boredom within, they are surprised that this interior world nourishes them. These are not people who have ever been easily engaged by life inside. They always had met either an empty and inhospitable isolation or the busy activity of self-assessment and analysis. But when they can experience their emotional life in its dimensions, interiority loses its terror. Quietism—inner blankness—fades and contemplation becomes something real and desirable.

Focusing in the formal sense as it is described by Eugene Gendlin[1] makes accessible this interior presence so needed by 2/3/4s. Focusing is particularly helpful because it utilizes the body function, and it is the body to which 2/3/4s have ready access. The physical organism yields much information for them. By reflecting on its messages, they can touch feelings. This process is another way of saying that the auxiliary function of reflective perception can reveal the hidden function of emotion. In focusing, a contemplative approach to the organism and its language of energy is described. Of course, as Gendlin himself has said, anyone who is self-reflective at all knows how to focus and practices this way of inner attention. However, the attitude, approach, and emphasis on requesting information about experience from their body function, which formal focusing describes, often helps 2/3/4s to deepen and expand periods of contemplation.

Since concentration on the physical organism is so instinctive for 2/3/4s, other approaches to self-awareness and self-knowledge that include this aspect can be fruitful. Listening and responding to music—even creating it, since 2/3/4s are by nature doers—can move them into feelings. Yoga makes a statement with the body they can read more readily than they can read emotions. To sit well is to pray well, as Zen asserts; action and inner life are one, and interior conditions are readable from the body and its symbolic postures and activities. Extended experiences of yoga reveal the reality of life within to 2/3/4s.

> The best thing that happened to me when I took up yoga was that I came to like myself for the first time. I felt I knew me and I was good. Something about assuming those postures or *asanas* and staying in them made a statement to me of my beauty and goodness and value.

Bioenergetic exercises and creative movement allow the body to speak its needs, concerns, and history. Even more important, the feelings that the body has stored become available once again, and 2/3/4s get acquainted with themselves by allowing expression of these feelings. They remain doers; they always need to externalize and express what is going on inside of them. They come to learn that they must express themselves primarily for their own information. Once they have so expressed themselves, they can choose what is important to express to others as well.[2]

Another body approach that helps 2/3/4s know who they are is massage. Allowing themselves to be cared for and tended opens to them their needs, makes them present in the moment, and gradually changes their attitude toward their body. They begin to consider this body less as a useful beast of burden and more as a companion who requires care and who instructs them about themselves. The body also makes them aware of their own reality amid the distractions of the external environment. It is interesting to note how many 2/3/4s instinctively turn to massage because of its benefits, verifying the bioenergetic theory that experience of "dis-ease" in the organism carries with it the knowledge of a way to growth and health.[3]

Motion of some kind nearly always accompanies self-presence for 2/3/4s. Being in mentally non-involved activity removes that top layer of anxiety nearly always present for them. Freed from anxiety and yet mentally available because their activity is something simple and repetitive, they grow less intense and ready to be surprised; their attitude is more contemplative. Housework, walking, driving the car along a familiar route may be involving enough to move 2/3/4s from striving for some interior goal to allowing whatever comes.

Since play for 2/3/4s is usually some activity, it is helpful for them to define leisure as "doing what I feel like doing." Reading their own desires, noticing their own energies, and allowing response to them is the way they learn leisure. It is also practice in discernment and decision-making regarding other of life's calls.

> A few years ago I wouldn't even have known what it was to enjoy a day off. Now I ask myself what would be my choice as to how to spend this time that is my own. Frankly, it's sometimes just to catch up on things I have to do, but at the leisurely pace I'd like to do them. Sometimes it's to go to the mall and try on clothes or have lunch with a friend. I couldn't have answered the question of what I might want for myself until recent times. So I guess I know myself better than I used to.

The compulsive deception that they are completely responsible for their environment makes it especially important for 2/3/4s to spend periods of time away from their everyday scene. They forget things they have to do only when those things are not around to haunt them. When they get away from familiar places with real or imagined expectations that exist there, they can be "on vacation," emptied out, as it were, of daily cares and concerns and able to attend to inner movements of their own emotions and energies.

Nature appeals to everyone. Its special invitation to 2/3/4s is that it places no demands, no necessity to perform. Neither does nature have any needs that call for attention. Nature simply is as it is. It asks for nothing, and this encourages 2/3/4s to be simply who they are. When nature is harmonious it speaks of the goodness and unity of creation; when it is in upheaval or conflict, it speaks of created reality with its problems and issues. Nature reflects and symbolizes the beauty as well as the limited aspect of all creation.

We have already noted how much activity and people constitute life for 2/3/4s. Early on they exaggerated this instinct to compulsion. As they become more enlightened and aware, they tend to distrust activity and to resist the emotion of anxiety, which of its nature thrusts them into action. And yet, it is this outer arena where they function well and where their strengths are manifest. Slowing to a stop in order to meditate and spending long periods of time alone and away from people will never become their way to wholeness. Life for them will always be found in relationship, but now it can include relationship with the self and the interior world as well as the outer one.

Going away from others is only valid if it results in a quality of self-presence that meets the Divine there and flows outside once again to other people. If it does not result in increased contemplation, it is merely narcissistic preoccupation. Those who are 2/3/4s will probably spend less time alone than other people do, because to be who they are will necessarily lead them into what is most vital for them: relationships. These relationships increasingly will be a communion of presence instead of a connection made up of activity.

When they touch into their affective lives rather than merely talk about having an affective life, they become less preoccupied with their spiritual progress and prayer, and often speak of it very little. They move from unconsidered, compulsive doing to a phase of conscious reflection on who they have become and who they need to become in the future. Beyond that period is one of simple and unselfconscious being. Once again, as de Mello has said, they need to look no further than the trees and sky and grass around them, but now it is because of their interior unity rather than their scatteredness.

One of the helps for 2/3/4s in this process is journaling, which involves keeping some written record of experience. Journaling needs to be done in a way consonant with who they are. They learn to be suspicious of a beautifully written, well-illustrated, neatly kept journal. A journal that has become a project or an art piece is one which comes from compulsion rather than spontaneous and genuine life. Probably for 2/3/4s, who need to be taken up into—or down into, if you will—what they feel, any place to spill out their energy will do. A journal that takes them beyond reflection on experience to experiencing in the moment is the best kind.

> My journal is full of four-letter words and I can hardly read what I write there. I just let my anger pour out and I often just tear out the pages after I've scribbled them, partly because I can't read them anyway and partly because I feel more free if I know nobody will ever see them. This allows me to let go of the censor inside and I rage. I rage a lot these days. God, does it have energy and strength for me. My journal? It's an old spiral notebook with pages gouged out by my poison pen or else ripped out and thrown away.

The helps 2/3/4s turn to along their way to contemplation will always be ones that bring them home to self. From that center they instinctively move out again, now in strength and virtue rather than in compulsion. How do they learn whether they have stayed in the cell of their hearts long enough? Only in the response or lack of it from those who are life/Life for them. Interactions with others tell them when and how and how often to seek that inner companion who is lovable, who is the self, who becomes their gift to offer.

Day by Day: Helps Toward Contemplation for 5/6/7s

Since 5/6/7s live so much of their lives within, the journey outward is their way to balance. It is only by touching into the fire of their own hearts—their emotional lives—that they find the urge to spill out and overflow from their instinctive inner world. Jesus, who lived and moved and had his being in this created universe, models the way they must immerse themselves in creation: self as well as others, persons as well as things.

The prayer of dialogue—of conversation with the Divine under some image or symbol, or with holy persons, or even with external objects that stand for interior realities—moves 5/6/7s into relationship. It may be a flower or a crucifix or a lighted candle that becomes the focus for attention. Guiding perceptions to a central one solves their problem of multiple options for meditation and keeps them from wandering down a multitude of interior perceptual pathways. Approaching prayer with open eyes also serves as a reminder that the exterior world exists. Not only does this candle or icon have being, but 5/6/7s need to remember that they too have a life outside themselves and experience personal to them.

> I forget to go outside. One thought leads to another and just collecting them and lining them up keeps me occupied. Planning liturgy with the people I live with gives me a time every week when I'm forced to express what I think and feel and then do something about it like choose a symbol or arrange flowers or bake bread. That way I'm less likely to float off and get lost in my own world.

Prayer of intercession is one extension of this dialogical approach to spirituality. It is good for 5/6/7s to ask the Other for what they need, to express concerns and speak in their own and others' behalf to the Divine. This putting words on their reality can become an effective way for 5/6/7s to keep a journal. To write down what they want to say, and then to respond to these statements helps articulation and breaks the ever-spinning inner circle of perception. Some 5/6/7s find it helpful to keep their entire journal in the form of letters to God or to some wisdom figure or to the child of their own personal history. Whoever the recipient of this fictional correspondence may be, the reminder of a world outside flows from it. Beyond a mere reminder is the personalizing of communication; they are no longer recounting experience but telling the one addressed about that experience as it happens.

With Jesus as a model in this regard, as in so many others, 5/6/7s learn to pray conversationally with the Creator God. Jesus prayed this way to his Father, asking for his needs to be cared for moment by moment. The bread of life/Life was a daily bread, not given all at once and stored away, but fresh bread like the manna of the Old Testament. Faith reminds 5/6/7s that future moments will have their own nourishment. The Creator in heaven never abandons offspring, but accompanies them through temptation and frees them from evils along their path.

The mere perception of being known by God can be turned into an actual experience of being known in various ways for 5/6/7s. An expansive but unshared interior life is a product of compulsion, so times when the inner person is expressed are essential to conversion. Reminders of the reality that God participates in human life can come especially through reading and savoring the gospel stories of Jesus' words and works. Scriptural passages such as Psalm 139, where the poet highlights unsuccessful attempts to find some place where God is not and where one cannot be found, underline significant 5/6/7 themes. Making music—singing or playing songs and hymns and making the feelings of this art form personal ones—helps them move interior considerations into outer expression.

Perhaps the most graphic way to reveal oneself is to be naked. Praying without body covering can be especially symbolic for instinctively private people like 5/6/7s. Clothes cover bodies and protect them from the elements. When 5/6/7s let themselves be revealed in their entirety they give away their secrets; they are vulnerable. Such stripping and allowing themselves to be open to God in prayer is both frightening and salutary for them as a statement of trust in the provident Creator who already sees and loves. It is a symbolic statement of intimacy and trust. It is also a reminder that the body is significant to experience and that the organism must be involved in spiritual life. Without the entire organism there can be no real human prayer.

The body can give other information to 5/6/7s when it is invoked. Walking slowly, they learn God leads them step by step. Praying with face pressed against the floor, they realize they are dependent on a God who provides. When they breathe deeply and take in the surrounding atmosphere and expand into the environment with each exhalation, they learn to let go to their outer world.

There may be some 5/6/7s who find creative movement helpful; however, more people in this space probably turn to bodily postures rather than motion to express themselves. Especially early in the conversion process, when they are still functioning largely from an instinct that pulls away and exaggerates perception, 5/6/7s find free bodily expression difficult. Awareness of an experience that is accompanied by continual movement is frequently impossible at that phase. Assuming some still posture allows organismic involvement and a reminder of the outer world even as it prevents the distraction involved in continual physical movement.

> When I'm sitting in meditation I often open my hands in my lap and look at them, palms up. They say, "Here I am as I am. I need you. Help me." But the words aren't even necessary. The open hands say it all. Just looking at them is my prayer beyond content of any kind.

Vocal prayer and chanting also bring what is inside outside for 5/6/7s. Such praying can be done alone or in community, where it is either liturgical worship or some other form of shared prayer. Reading their journal entries aloud, an approach recommended by Ira Progoff in his Intensive Journal Workshop,[4] makes them more concrete because it articulates their experiences. Simply sitting with and listening to themselves symbolically states that they are valuable and worthy of attention, that they deserve respect for what they say and do as well as for what they perceive.

As for all enneagram spaces—that is, for all human beings— nature draws 5/6/7s to God. The physical sensations of touch, taste, smell, and hearing allow them to feast on creation beyond merely observing it. To feel the texture of a rose petal, brush the covering of a peach, smell an herb garden, or taste some beverage enlarges the experience of creation and celebrates it more fully. It also brings the inner outside to action.

Another contribution nature offers 5/6/7s is an experience of the vastness and power of creation manifested in broad expanse, high mountains, wide bodies of water. This immensity of nature pulls them out of themselves and into its vastness. They are drawn into a whole greater than themselves, but of which they are a significant part. They see their limited finiteness against a backdrop which is huge but not threatening or overpowering.

The basic symbol of food and nourishment for life's journey, which Jesus chose to leave and which he himself became, assumes special significance for 5/6/7s. They learn to take and eat, not once and for all, but again and again along their way to God. By assimilating the words of scripture and the Word who is Jesus himself, they gain strength to meet whatever may arise with courageous power. They take into themselves and are transformed by the Son, in whose power they live and move and are.

Prayer for 5/6/7s usually holds something of reflective meditation, since instinctively they view life from their mental function. To be truly prayer, however, it must include affect that carries it beyond merely dry, empty, and emotionless perceptions of reality. As they learn how easily they can be lost in the perceptions, enlightened 5/6/7s find themselves approaching the object of their meditation with a more relaxed attitude. They are better able to circle around and savor the focus of their meditation. Eventually they fall into its mysterious dimension beneath mere externals. Sensations and other bodily responses, as well as personal memories and experience, extend their instinctive perceptual response to a more total organismic one involving emotion and energy.

> I was great at re-creating the whole gospel scene when I meditated. But there was no meat on the people in the stories. My Jesus had no heart or soul, let alone a body. That was probably because I didn't either. Things are better now that I've become more than a walking head. Jesus is alive now and in my real life and so am I, increasingly so.

As 5/6/7s live into their days, one at a time, they relax some of the boundaries separating them from other people and their environment. As they learn to value themselves, they accept others' valuing of them. They see their surroundings in a more friendly way. Out of this self-value and self-worth they risk opening what they have come to recognize as inner treasures to other people, knowing that in the sharing these will not be diminished or exhausted, but rather enhanced.

Loving Attention: Helps Toward Contemplation for 8/9/1s

The great gift of the 8/9/1s is their ability to simply be present in the moment. It is also possible for them to grow sleepy and inattentive, for the continuum with contemplation as one pole has inertia as its opposite. Here, more than in any other enneagram stance, we find a capacity to be taken by and taken up into whatever each successive moment holds. This is the enneagram stance most characteristically existential.

The prayer spiritual writers call loving attention most naturally belongs to 8/9/1s. When they pray in their most instinctive and gifted way, they are simply present before God as they are.

This presence involves no thinking, feeling, or moving. It is a still and uncluttered centering reached by emptying and letting go of their wants and desires, pleasures and satisfactions. Beyond all of these diverse energies is the peaceful, joyful pulling down of life energy into the ground of being. Here in the body center, the *hara*—that place beneath the navel where all comes to balance—the Ground of Being unifies them.

This centered place is not vague and dreamy. Present there, 8/9/1s move out of perceptual lethargy and into a state of alertness. Although they know it is not laziness, they are loathe to describe anything that happens in this place. They only know that they move on from it refreshed and with boundaries relaxed within them and between themselves and others. It is the place beyond the war and its battles where peace reigns and all manner of life is accessible.

> Every morning after breakfast I take my cup of coffee to my desk and just sit there looking out of the window. But I'm not looking out of the window. I'm just sitting there with myself and God and my day. Time disappears. Before you know it, forty minutes or an hour have gone by. I wouldn't trade that time for anything, but I'd be at a loss to make a case for why I should keep on doing it. Maybe I could say it gets me into gear. My day becomes mine and I'm God's and everything adds up somehow. But that doesn't say it either. Nothing seems to.

People in the 8/9/1 space who move into life's second task become aware of their pervasive tendency toward inertia. When it becomes compulsive, this instinct leads them either to follow a line of least resistance or else to insist that others carry the efforts of any endeavors in which they become mutually involved. Observing their dynamic can cause them to be suspicious of effortless prayer. They feel they are doing nothing; they judge themselves lazy. If observations turn into self-condemnation, they of course move away from self and prayer. If they try to replace simple presence to God and God to them with some sort

of content, they frustrate their natural flow and their genuine
prayer energy.

It is also true that this simple presence evaporates as soon as
they try to evaluate its quality and measure what is going on.
Such self-observation comes less from an exaggerated activity
function, as it would for 2/3/4s, and more from the fear of
losing control of self, of disappearing or drowning or getting
sucked into the intense whirlpool which is life/Life—one's own
and the Divine. They wonder whether, were they to surrender
too easily and too completely, they would ever get back to
themselves and their needs and endeavors. Perhaps they would
cease to be themselves and lose their identity in the Divine. It
is no small matter to engage the living God, as scripture has
warned. They do so only in the belief that this God respects
their persons and desires relationship rather than annihilation.

The constant resistance to flow, the battle within and outside
that engages so much 8/9/1 energy, comes as much from fear
as from anger. Their aggression, whether it be overt or covert,
often covers fright that insists on protective parameters. If God
is energy, where does mine end and God's begin? Who am
I? Am I anyone? The tendency to merge with surroundings
and persons reaches its ultimate terror in the prayer relationship
with God.

Helps to contemplation for 8/9/1s all possess the theme of
assuring them that they are people in their own right, and that
surrender to the flow of Life Energy, which is the Divine,
is their choice to make and will not wipe out their existence.
Prayer of the body serves as an effective reminder to 8/9/1s that
they have personal boundaries and that they can move beyond
them if they choose to do so. Yoga postures, creative movement,
acting out in mime a story or myth or scriptural passage or
dream are some ways to underline the reality of a self they can
choose to surrender. This reminder and assurance of existence
allows them to trust being taken up and beyond themselves.
Such back and forth from awareness to action eventually stills
to simple presence.

Zazen, sitting alert yet relaxed before reality, symbolizes the gathering of all their functions—indeed, of their complete organism—into unity. In this posture they allow successive moments to stream past, neither grasping at them to hurry focus and clarity nor hanging on to them to keep them alive. This zen practice helps them experience presence to, rather than judgment about, reality. There is no editing of this moment to moment flow; what is outside pours easily inside and what is inside moves out.

Suppression of judgment is one of the gifts that being in nature offers 8/9/1s. The Creator holds all at once, themselves included, and sees that all is good. One loving and unified creation and their place in that totality becomes their experience. Beginnings, middles, ends are all seen as segments of the whole. Important stands out from less important and takes proper position; they can assume their own place relative to everything else. Life takes on new perspective. Creation pulsates as a single unit.

The world of the image and symbol, which is how the unconscious speaks to us, is especially revealing to 8/9/1s. They speak and think symbolically, which means by way of analogy. Many of these symbols are taken from nature. This fact often needs to be pointed out to them, because they tend to overlook or dismiss the significance of such communications. While all people find the stories of humankind as expressed in myth and folklore helpful in highlighting their reality, 8/9/1s especially need this approach to gather perceptions and come to insight and meaning. With their perceptual function so inaccessible, they often strive for a logic that is distant from this innate approach to knowing. Image, symbol, and myth lead them through their feelings without denying them until they arrive at clarity of perception.

Using their bodies in order to find insight and meaning, order, and perspective is also a very effective way of praying for 8/9/1s. Adding activity to their symbolic world by graphically reproducing it using paint or clay or some other medium of expression helps them. Working with their symbolic life bridges inner and outer and links the two. They need help joining this inner and outer. Action brings together involvement with the symbol and provides enough distance to reduce fear of being immersed or overwhelmed by what the symbol opens up for them.

> I got in touch with this inner Judge who hates me and beats me up. I shrank when I first saw him in my imagination the way I do when he abuses me. I could see he was ugly and I could feel his meanness. I was paralyzed, just couldn't do anything. Then I drew a picture of him and eventually was able to write about who he is and what he does and how I feel about him. Then I talked to him, finally, and got to know him. I need to bring him back some more times. He needs to hear me, and I want to tell him where I am and what I want of him. Not being so afraid, I think I can do that better now.

The world of asleep and awake dreams is one of images and symbols.[5] Often these dreams are especially fruitful for contemplation because they are specific to the individual. Whether 8/9/1s follow a spontaneous image or whether someone or something has suggested an image for their meditation, the learnings can be rich. One reason for the power in this approach is that 8/9/1s are more inclined than others to become involved in images and symbols rather than maintaining a safe but self-conscious detachment from them. Working with these dream images by questions, associations, amplifications, body response, and other forms of dreamwork is a way of noticing, honoring, and attending to this rich world of perceptual revelation.

One established dream theory states that dreams are statements from the unconscious that fill out information about reality beyond what one is already conscious of. The dream acts as a negative of conscious experience. What is bright and clear on a photo print is dark on the photographic negative and vice versa; bright areas of a photographic negative are the dark areas in the printed photo. Applying this image to dream theory, it would seem that the least accessible, most denied, and underdeveloped function would be the one to be especially attentive to when looking at one's dreams.

How does this apply to enneagram considerations? For 2/3/4s the emotional function in the dream is the first place to focus; that is, the feelings that are present during the dream and after waking. 5/6/7s can focus on the decisions and actions the dream characters encountered: the options that confronted them and what they did at these turning points. For 8/9/1s, coming to insights from perceptual connections suggests they use various approaches in working with dream images. For example, they might name the persons and objects in the dream, freely associating around the dream elements, speaking to these elements, filling out connections between the dream and previous awake experience.

The energy pulling back and forth, inside and out, which so characterizes 8/9/1s, calls them to responsible focus and from that focus into action. Their spiritual life needs a discipline of concentration amid the diverse energies pulling them in opposite directions. The conceptualization of God as Other helps 8/9/1s move out from the world inside themselves with its needs and desires and wishes and satisfactions to a world of other people and the Divine. Any method to help active contemplation that includes both inner and outer elements facilitates this movement, ultimately making it so smooth a passageway that going from inside to outside is flowing rather than difficult.

Communal prayer, especially of a liturgical nature, can help 8/9/1s in the struggle toward surrender to these inner and outer polarities. Cooperating with their personal energy in group prayer calls for its own kind of surrender. Chanting in a more private and individual setting, such as using a mantra or reading psalmody or other scripture aloud, can also underline the realities of both interior and exterior and unite them. One symbolic form of prayer that highlights the poles of activity and passivity

found in contemplation is the gradual shortening of a verbal-
ized mantra or scripture passage until there remains only silence.
This silence, as a still point of energetic focus, carries into the
day's other activities, readying 8/9/1s for its surprises.

Journal keeping for 8/9/1s helps them do what they most
need to do: see their emotions, issues, and bodily responses
as aspects of themselves rather than as all of their being. When
they write down an experience, it becomes something they can
observe and explore from a more objective place. Journaling
also serves to help them remember happenings of their lives
they are prone to forget. Especially intense feeling around a
memory often obliterates it entirely from their awareness. To
have it written down as it occurred marks its time and place
and gives it an existence to return and attend to with the care it
warrants. This conscious attention prevents carrying the burden
of undigested past experience into the present and feeling its
oppression.

Finally, journaling entries reviewed from time to time point
out patterns and rhythms and causality that can be helpful in
present response. Such a panorama from past to now provides
a perspective 8/9/1s do not instinctively have.

> I don't write much in my journal. It would take me weeks to
> tell you everything that I was going through this morning. So
> I usually draw a picture. The lines, the colors, not to mention
> the content of what I draw and the medium I use, all capture
> what happened on one page in a better way than words could
> ever do. I say everything in one graphic statement.

The Place of Discernment in Active Contemplation

If we define active contemplation as readying ourselves for
the gift which is presence—our own, another's, God's—then
the enneagram becomes an important help in this process.
When we know our instinctive approach to life, how we have
compulsively exaggerated it, and yet how it alone is meant to
be our primary gift to creation, we have a valuable backdrop
of experiential information against which to read our energies.

Based on this awareness, we learn contemplative presence; we discern genuine from false energy.

One application of how self-knowledge assists discernment is the way we approach our past. Individual life history forms a major part of everyone's spiritual journey. The way we incorporate significant elements of that story into present experience, however, varies depending on our stance in life. The way to invite from the unconscious those aspects of the past that are relevant in this present moment differs for the three basic stances. What helps one space is either inaccessible or compulsive—and therefore deceptive and false—for another.

For 2/3/4s, who have such difficulty in allowing present emotions, anything that takes them on an intellectual trip or a reporting of past experience only pulls them further from the moment. Their most helpful way to view their history is to allow present emotions fully and then relax and reflect on, rather than analyze, when they knew such feelings in the past. To put this in an image, it is as though they follow the feelings experienced in the present backward in a pathway until that particular feeling is recognized in their past history. A chronological or thematic re-creation of their entire life story is counterproductive. It turns into another task that pulls them out of relevant present experience.

For 5/6/7s, however, a conscious re-creation of their history can serve to honor it, to make real again the person who felt what they felt, dreamed what they dreamed, loved whom they loved, struggled as they struggled. The important aspect of this story, of course, is that it includes affective elements around these memories, that it be a story which values feelings, respects efforts, reminds them of their own care for others and others for them. The precious truth of who they are and who others are to them underlines their significance as persons. Because their emotional function is accessible, is their auxiliary function, it helps in this process.

For 8/9/1s their history may be most effectively, because less threateningly, remembered analogically. Similes and metaphors shape and form emotion-laden memories imaginatively and symbolically. The objective but engaged attention of this approach helps them address in small segments the accumulated baggage of past experience. They can taste, nibble, savor, ruminate on their stories piece by piece. As they do this, more and more of this past is offered them from a shy and frightened unconscious, which hid away what was too much for them to deal with at the time it happened.

We have already discussed various emphases dream work might involve depending on a person's enneagram space. We have spoken, too, of a journaling approach for each enneagram stance. Once one knows one's space on the circle of human creation, this knowledge becomes an important factor in facilitating discernment of genuine from compulsive energies. We gradually learn as we grow in enlightenment to name and call forth those energies which are life-giving. At the same time we become friendly toward, and yet disciplined concerning, those energies we once thought helpful but later learned we had overemphasized and colored with illusion and delusion.

We learn this discernment only through trial and error. Such an educational method fits our human condition. Like Adam and Eve, we as children were exiled from our Garden for the purpose of learning. Life experience teaches us better than anything else.

One thing we learn is that no amount of preparation to receive the flow of life/Life will ever cause that flow; life is freely given. We are transformed through the process of living into being wise people. Wisdom makes us humble, relaxed with our human condition, responsive to self and others and God. The wise wait patiently in the moment for the light/Light and life/Life. They can do no more.

CHAPTER 11

The Enneagram: A Help to Contemplation

The enneagram is an oral tradition. Because this is so, it is difficult to pinpoint individuals who originated specific reflections on the theory. It is also hard to stop the unfolding of idea upon idea, example after example, once the seed of some new perception has been planted.[1] Those who live with awareness of the enneagram recognize the temptation to fascination as some small observation opens up and begins to grow, evolving as it does so. It is hard to draw boundaries of topic and subtopic when writing about this constantly revealing approach to the human person. It is even more difficult for a writer to end the discussion, knowing it has just begun. Are there some final considerations to be mentioned or underlined again so that, having closed this book, the reader may carry it into life?

One question that often arises asks how the study of the enneagram relates to Christian spirituality. How does it tie into theological studies about sin and grace and theory and doctrine surrounding these issues? What relationship is there between descriptions of the nine points, individual dynamics, and living as a Christian?

For those who see the Christian life as keeping rules and holding doctrines, there is no answer to these questions. The enneagram merely takes its place beside other personality descriptions to be evaluated for its accuracy and invoked to clarify

157

human personality. Enneagram vocabulary becomes just another way to talk about the structure of the person.

Human life, spiritual life, is dynamic and contemplative. It can only be lived by people who already have plunged, or at least desire to plunge, themselves into its stream. Such people are willing to risk drowning rather than continue their dry existence on the bank alongside the flow of living water. The enneagram reveals to them what it means to feel as though they are drowning—and yet inexplicably to survive.

Only contemplatives will truly understand the enneagram, because only contemplatives have lived life fully enough to taste the rancid waters of their compulsions without spitting it out. Only contemplatives are courageous enough to swallow from the stream, get used to its taste, and believe refreshment comes from drinking what promises only bitterness or tastelessness or sickness, and yet when purified gives energy.

For those who know they must fall into living waters, the enneagram offers continual nourishment. They can know and name and experience sinfulness and evil with considerations the enneagram clarifies and places in context. They can learn about the injustice toward self and others and God that occurred when they created a merciless Divine figure. They come to realize all that people have done, and they must undo this injustice or perpetuate their own slavery. They experience aspects of the Divine because they experience aspects of self and others that reveal that Divine.

Tasting one's creatureliness, powerlessness, frustration, and anxiety about death—physical and otherwise—is essential for spiritual awareness and growth, for active and passive contemplative experience to happen. The enneagram uncovers what one has hidden, suggests what one has denied, promises what one thought impossible—being recognized as good by one's self. Such recognition extends to respect for others and for God. Humility, the foundation and bulwark of spiritual traditions through the ages, is the fruit of experiencing personal realities the enneagram names and describes.

An ever-yielding source of information about the enneagram wells up, but this information always centers around the theme of knowing and accepting creatureliness and a Creator. One final reflection, one additional gazing into this mystery, concludes this book.

For this reflection I have chosen to write in the language of the unconscious, because it is through the unconscious becoming conscious that we learn about our own lives and the lives of other people. The unconscious, upon invitation, speaks to us of what is so for us. It is the companion of our contemplative lives, yielding little by little its hidden, dark areas to the light of life/Life.

The unconscious speaks primarily in images. Because it does so, and because we often understand it best in this symbolic vocabulary, I have chosen to summarize and underline the theme of enneagram spirituality—or human growth, conversion, individuation, enlightenment, rebirth, or however else we translate being alive—in reflections on an art song by the contemporary writer Leonard Cohen.[2] In doing so I follow a long tradition in writing about spirituality. This tradition includes images of Benedict's ladder of humility, Teresa of Avila's interior mansions, and John of the Cross' ascent of the mountain. It also includes Ignatius' two battle standards and Thérèse of Lisieux's little way.

"Joan of Arc" tells the story of the young soldier-saint from an interior perspective rather than a historical one. Cohen expresses poetically what these pages have described in prose. The entire experience of his message requires music along with the text.

"Joan of Arc," the Enneagram, and the Spiritual Path

> Oh, the flames they followed Joan of Arc
> As she came riding through the dark.

More than one spiritual writer has chosen fire and flame to speak of how human beings experience God. Fire burns and destroys things as they are, transforming them from the elements that make them up into something radically different. This being true, the results of fire's transformation presuppose some substance with which to interact.

So, too, we are transformed by God's action in our lives, by our particular existence encountering Existence. The form and content of our personal self, natively endowed and developed by learnings and circumstances, becomes someone who exists only because the original material was what it was. We can be only that creation we were meant to be; we can offer only that gift of particular incarnation for which we have the potential. The flames of God's light and love come only to someone riding, albeit through the dark; God seeks for someone in the process of human growth, not an empty void.

> No moon to keep her armor bright,
> No man to get her through this dark and smoky night.

In this song Joan is clearly at the point of life's second task. Her protective armor, the boundaries she has set up to hold herself away from self-awareness and to protect her from others, has lost its former glitter. Even when her armor shone, it did so not in daylight but in a dim world lit by the meager light of the moon, itself a body only imitating brightness and clarity. The moon has no genuine and interior source of light. Yet, even this moonlight has gone away.

The moment of conversion comes for all of us when we are no longer able to maintain the image of ourselves that once contented us. Nothing can make this distorted image look true or bright or genuine. We recognize we live in a dark world. No distractions or lies or exaggerated positive images or even distorted pictures of enforced victimization any longer enlighten our way or satisfy us. Nothing outside or within ourselves offers comfort. We are alone and we stand facing the false and manufactured cover with which we hid our individual existence and our personal responsibility.

She said, "I'm tired of the war.
I want the kind of work I had before.
A wedding dress—or something white—
To wear upon my swollen appetite."

The process of conversion is an essential part of human development if we are to fulfill our human destiny. We are created to be contemplative enough for confronting the illusions and distortions, the delusions and false assessments by which we hide from what we cannot face. Because we judged our naked truth to be beyond anyone's embrace, we learned to lie, hoping that this lie would make us lovable, would attract someone into helping us belong to the human community. We try to recapture again our contentment with the false view that made us appear adequate, competent, successful, worthy of attention, wise, friendly, good, just. If we can go back to that image, we tell ourselves, we will recover the life we knew before this dark conflict settled in.

Instead, we continue to see our exaggerated and distorted instinct, enlarged to excess, disproportionately swollen. We look for that illusion of the lovableness we strove so hard to gain, but it is gone. In its place we find only pervasive appetite: our overused anxious activity, our hyper-perceptivity, our rampant or denied emotion. We face the instinct we covered over by attempting to make someone we and others could find desirable or at least tolerable. Now we see how these efforts have only enslaved us in unyielding and binding, limiting and cold armor. We have lost our freedom, our very being, in our efforts to belong.

"Well, I'm glad to hear you talk this way.
I've watched you riding every day."

There may be no more lonely moment in life than the one which tells us how misguided our attempts at living have been. Yet it is only at this moment that God, who is Truth and Life, can begin to engage us at a new and deeper and necessary level. Only when we have exhausted our efforts to make ourselves

into the people we think it well to be can we hear the voice
of Truth, Integrity, and Authenticity from inside us. This voice
is the voice of life/Life, and it calls us beyond past deception
and present despair. It invites encounter because it says "I have
looked upon you and you are good" (Gn 1). It is the voice
of our deepest word where we find the Word of God. It is
experienced throughout our whole organism, speaking louder
than the lies we have shouted at ourselves to drown it out.

> "And there's something in me that yearns to win
> such a cold, such a lonesome heroine."

The wonder of the spiritual journey is that only when we
have developed a strong enough ego based on our distorted
function of body, perception, or emotion—our exaggerated
anxiety, fear, or anger or our buried anger, anxiety, or fear—
can this encounter with life/Life take place. It does so at the
level of presence to self, others, and the Creator. Our compulsions become our shame; they also lead us to the only glory we
can offer the Creator.

> "And who are you?" she sternly spoke
> To the one beneath the smoke.
> "Why, I'm fire," he replied,
> "And I love your solitude, and I love your pride."

Encounter with life/Life is not something any of us wel-
comes except in theory. The reality of risk, of letting ourselves become aware of what we have forgotten—our pride,
deceit, or envy; our avarice, fear, or gluttony; our lust, sloth,
or resentment—makes life seem undesirable. We realize that our
distorted self-image, originally as bright as a wedding dress, was
woven only at the price of self-imprisonment. This false image
must be burned away.

The fires of authenticity, truth, and integrity have become
our awesome partners. Small wonder that we are often discour-
aged, depressed, disillusioned, and perhaps even shamed when
we first hear ourselves described in enneagram terms. But still,

our word, beneath the smoke of our deceptions, invites us to communion.

> "Well, then, fire, make your body cold,
> I'm going to give you mine to hold."
> And saying this she climbed inside
> To be his one, to be his only bride.

We enter into life. Amid the trials and errors, the foolishness and wisdom, the laziness and effort, we discover who we are with searing brightness. We learn that all the advice from other people about the way to God must be sifted and sorted in relation to our own experience. This experience is based on our instinctive perception of life. We may realize that a suggestion which urges us out of ourselves is a dangerous siren song. We may discover that someone who tells us just to stay within reinforces our evil. We may come to know that we need both to protect ourselves and let ourselves go, however that may happen.

There is no other way to God than by living beyond the ignorance from which we committed our fundamental sin into the trial and error of experiential education that leads us to become wise concerning self, others, and the Divine. We sometimes get busy, run away, go to sleep, but once on this pathway it becomes harder and harder to reverse the process. We can only delay it, and delay it we do. We profess our commitment to life/Life, but on our terms: life/Life must not hurt too much; it must not cost too much; it must adapt to our limitations.

> Then deep into his fiery heart
> He took the dust of Joan of Arc,
> And high above all these wedding guests
> He hung the ashes of her lovely wedding dress.

Life does its work. Eventually we no longer see ourselves with the deceptions our ego created. We know ourselves in ever-increasing reality, and in this knowing relax more and more into who we are. We let others see us too. There is no longer any need to hide away. We admit our anger, our anxiety, our fear. We begin to realize that others, and our Creator most completely, always knew at least some of what we could not allow our judgmental selves to know.

Because we now no longer feel compelled to hide our reality away or cover it over with exaggerated aspects of ourselves we judge more attractive and desirable, we are less distorted. Our functions come into balance. We no longer hold off our energy in our head or skeleton or heart. We fall into our center. We wear a wedding dress we at first did not like and realize it not only fits, but it is becoming. Instead of wanting the white and perfect covering of perfection, we are clothed in ashes and we come to accept these ashes as our most appropriate wedding gown. This covering symbolizes that the fire of life/Life itself has transformed us into a bride we at first did not want to be. We have opened to life; we have become receptive and responsive as every spouse must become if the joy of union is to take place.

> It was deep into his fiery heart
> He took the dust of Joan of Arc;
> And then she clearly understood:
> If he was fire, oh, then, she must be wood!

Life's lesson is one we all learn if we really live as human beings, as creatures of God. We become who we were meant to be: fallible and falling, living and learning. We reach this awareness whether or not we have ever heard of the enneagram. But as we meet day after day of our existence in this world, one of the ways to wholeness may come through the shining and clear—if necessarily confronting—description of us this theory offers. Such a description includes the hidden and unconscious area of our positive potential as well as of our limitation, at least as we so evaluate ourselves. It is precisely out of our innate dynamic that both develop. In fact, it is the interweaving of vice and virtue that creates the interesting, colorful fabric we are, and we learn as we grow in wisdom to appreciate that tapestry.

We come to see, too, that the Fire of Life has loved us in our brokenness and dividedness as well as in our wholeness.

> I saw her wince, I saw her cry;
> I saw the glory in her eye.

However it happens that we learn who we are, we have still another step on the spiritual pathway. That step leads us to embrace the one we have come to see, trusting in the lovable creation we are. Until we live beyond building up our character, beyond trying to incorporate into our personalities the virtues of the other enneagram points, we are still playing god. When we can both admit our limitations and vices and celebrate our strengths and virtues, we discover that life/Life itself and our wholehearted acceptance of it has shaped and formed us into the perfectly imperfect creation we were intended to be.

> Myself, I long for love and light,
> But must it come so cruel, must it be so bright?

There is only one way to wholeness or human maturity or whatever we choose to call it in whatever system we use to organize our perceptions about change and growth. The enneagram has proven to be one of the clearest and most enlightening ways for people to look at themselves and others with whom they live. If we use the enneagram as just another personality theory, it yields much valuable information for assisting self-appraisal and coming to self-awareness. At another and deeper level, however, the enneagram can assist conversion and transformation by radically confronting deception. It can reveal the depths of our evil, an evil which is not our instinct exaggerated into compulsion, but rather our lack of acceptance of this word that we are and that God has made. We can come to profound and salutary shame over refusing to accept who we are, and therefore denying the only reality we have to offer the God of Life.

It is true that even to recognize what the enneagram has to offer us we must already be contemplatives. Clearly, some level of contemplation is necessary to admit compulsion and the exaggerations and denials that early on seemed our only course. The enneagram offers us information on why we chose certain distortions as well as what particular contribution we can hope to make to human existence.

Finally, when we least expect, if we watch and wait for life/Life in present moments—all the time we can claim—the "dark lightning"[3] will move from illuminating our experience to blinding us. From then on, we will no longer need even to reflect or ponder any more. We will just live. The enneagram will no longer matter very much. Until that time, however, it has much to offer all who seek. ·

Endnotes

Introduction

1. A number of authors in recent years have written about the ancient wisdom of the enneagram as applied to the creation of human beings. I recommend Helen Palmer, *The Enneagram* (San Francisco: Harper and Row, 1988); Don Richard Riso, *Personality Types, Using the Enneagram for Self-Discovery* (Boston: Houghton Mifflin, 1987).

2. Aside from his own writings, the best articulation of Carl Jung's theory of individuation for me has been Jolande Jacobi's *The Way of Individuation* (New York: Meridian Books, New American Library, 1967).

3. Those familiar with the enneagram will note that I follow the theory of Oscar Ichazo, founder of the Arica Institute in New York. His approach is also found in Riso, *Personality Types*. A second theory has grown out of the work of Claudio Naranjo. Palmer, *The Enneagram*, is based in this latter approach.

4. For descriptions of personality found in this book I am most indebted to those with whom I have worked at The Institute for Spiritual Leadership of Loyola University of Chicago. The staff and participants of this community have over the years refined the descriptions of the nine incarnations of the human person. My primary gratitude goes to Paul V. Robb, S.J., who invited me to work with him and introduced me to the enneagram. While my approach to the enneagram differs from his, I wish to acknowledge the notes of Robert Ochs, S.J., which were my own introduction to this study.

Chapter 1

1. Sam Keen, *The Passionate Life, Stages in Loving* (San Francisco: Harper and Row, 1983), p. 250.

2. For an insightful and often humorous picture of how we as human beings divide and separate our experience, using the story of Adam and Eve, see Ken Wilber, *No Boundary* (Boulder: Shambhala, 1981), pp. 17–29.

3. Much of this and the following chapters began in my efforts to apply to my own course on contemplative attitude the materials of a course

on psychospiritual growth and development taught by Paul Robb, S.J. This latter course formed the core in The Institute for Spiritual Leadership curriculum. For an introduction to his thought, see *Studies in the Spirituality of Jesuits*, vol. 14, no. 3 (May 1982).

Chapter 2

1. Jacobi speaks about the various archetypes we use to describe this second task of life, including that of the Holy Saturday Liturgy of the Paschal Candle. For a description of the gravity of the process as expressed in image and symbol, see Jacobi, *The Way of Individuation*, "The Archetype of the Individuation Process."

2. Walt Disney's film "Fantasia" casts Mickey Mouse as this apprentice, who acts out the story to the musical score. His "performance" captures the growing agitation experienced when a person loses control of self and environment.

3. For the spirituality of Julian of Norwich as it applies to contemporary life, see Robert Llewelyn, *All Shall Be Well* (New York: Paulist Press, 1982).

4. Karlfried Graf von Durckheim, *The Way of Transformation* (London: George Allen and Unwin, 1985).

5. Abraham Maslow, *The Farther Reaches of Human Nature* (New York: Viking Press, 1971).

6. Jacobi, *The Way of Individuation*, "Conscious Realization."

7. Teresa of Avila, *The Interior Castle*, trans. Kieran Kavanaugh and Otilio Rodriguez (New York: Paulist Press, 1979).

Chapter 3

1. The book which for me has linked the physical aspects of the human being with psychospiritual development most insightfully is von Durckheim, *The Way of Transformation*. His discussion of how we all pull away from our center and dam up the flow of life as well as his identification of those places in our upper body to which we pull away are consonant with the enneagram as I have learned and experienced it.

2. See Suzanne Zuercher, O.S.B., "My Cat and Other Contemplative Surprises," *Praying*, no. 19 (May-June 1989); idem, "The Contemplative in Each of Us," *Living Prayer* (Jan.-Feb. 1990). The theme that underlies both of these articles is that the second task of life enables us to open

more and more to a reality we once did not have the personal strength to allow ourselves to see.

3. For this hopeful view of human development I am primarily indebted to the principles set forth in the client-centered therapy of Carl Rogers. I was introduced to this theory by Charles Arthur Curran, Ph.D., with whom I studied and worked for many years at Loyola University of Chicago. Father Curran insisted, as do other nondirective therapists, that interior resources are always present within the human person. He also taught that, instead of denying their basic personalities, people will go back through the same path by which they came; that is, they will find growth in and through those experiences which caused them problems in their development.

Chapter 4

1. I originally heard these post-resurrection stories applied to the three basic enneagram spaces in the mid–1970s when I began to work at The Institute for Spiritual Leadership. At that time they were already an accepted part of the oral tradition. This and the following two chapters comprise an extended meditation on Magdalene, Thomas, and Peter, as they embody the basic stances.

2. John 20:1–18. The story of Thomas is in John 20:19–29. Peter's story is told in John 21:15–23.

Chapter 7

1. I first heard this idea expressed by David Steindl-Rast in a lecture given to participants at The Institute for Spiritual Leadership in the late 1970s. I am especially grateful to him for his inquiries to me about how the Spirit is reflected in the lives of 2/3/4s. Because he urged me to put my experience into words, he inspired me to ask people in the other spaces about their experience of incarnating the other aspects of the Trinity. Although Brother David does not use enneagram terms, he has written a moving spiritual book on the virtues of faith, hope, and love and the contemplative life. See *Gratefulness, The Heart of Prayer* (New York: Paulist Press, 1984). Of particular value for those interested in the enneagram are the chapters "Faith and Beliefs," "Hope: Openness for Surprise," and "Love: a 'Yes' to Belonging."

2. Roberto Assagioli, *The Act of Will* (Baltimore: Penguin Books, 1974), p. 34.

3. For Merton's insights on the true and false self, see, in addition to his own writings, William Shannon, *Thomas Merton's Dark Path* (New York: Penguin Books, 1981); James Finley, *Merton's Palace of Nowhere* (Notre Dame, Indiana: Ave Maria Press, 1978); and Anne E. Carr, *A Search for Wisdom and Spirit* (Notre Dame, Indaina: University of Notre Dame Press, 1988).

4. Von Durckheim, *The Way of Transformation*, p. 102.

Chapter 8

1. James Nelson's book *Embodiment* (Minneapolis: Augsburg Press, 1978) has been influential for me in the way that it presents the human person as enfleshed, especially his section on the importance of sensuality (pp. 84–93). Sam Keen's books, *The Passionate Life: Stages of Loving* (New York: Harper and Row, 1983) and *To A Dancing God* (New York: Harper and Row, 1970) also bridge the gap often found between seeing the human person as flesh and spirit.

2. Paul Robb, S.J., and Mary Stuart, D.W., of The Institute for Spiritual Leadership have added much to my awareness and articulation of the 5/6/7 spaces. For insights and wording of the 8/9/1 approach to reality I am indebted to Patricia Coughlin, O.S.B., and Mary Melady, O.S.B., also of the Institute staff. Ann McElhatton, R.S.C.J., and I have worked together exploring our 2/3/4 experience.

3. For a discussion of surprise present in contemplation, see Steindl-Rast, *Gratefulness, The Heart of Prayer*.

4. Henri Nouwen, "The Journey from Despair to Hope," *Praying*, no. 17 (March/April, 1987).

5. For an introduction to how the posture and actions of the body mirror the personal history, life stance, and present attitude of a person, see Robert Masters and Jean Houston, *Listening to the Body* (New York: Delacorte Press, 1978); and Alexander and Leslie Lowen, *The Way to Vibrant Health* (New York: Harper Colophon Books, 1977).

Chapter 9

1. For a clear description of the kinesthetic experience of moving from ego to self—from the first task of life to the second—see Karlfried Graf von Durckheim, *Hara, The Vital Centre of Man* (London: Allen and Unwin, 1985), especially the chapter "The Order of Life in the Symbolism of the Body."

2. Alexander Lowen has described in detail the relationship between our present state and those emotional experiences we have locked away in our organism. His works include *Depression and the Body* (New York: Penguin Books, 1972); *The Language of the Body* (New York: Macmillan, 1974); and *The Betrayal of the Body* (New York: Macmillan, 1969).

3. Anthony de Mello, *One Minute Wisdom* (Garden City, New York: Doubleday Publishers, 1985), p. 47.

4. Roberto Assagioli speaks about "the energized I" and discusses the qualities of the person who is in touch with this flow of energy (*The Act of Will*). I am especially indebted to Roger Evans of the London Psychosynthesis Institute for clarifying Assagioli's theories during a workshop sponsored by the Canadian Psychosynthesis Institute in 1978. Both Assagioli's and Evans' presentations appear consonant with the theory of discernment described by St. Ignatius Loyola in his *Spiritual Exercises*.

5. See Riso, *Personality Types*, for the presentation of this theory. The longer I reflect on it, and the more I experience in my own life and in working with other people, the more I find it to be so.

6. For descriptions of the dynamics of each enneagram space, see, Palmer, *The Enneagram*, and Riso, *Personality Types*.

Chapter 10

1. Eugene Gendlin, *Focusing* (New York: Everest House, 1978).

2. For a simple introduction to creative movement, see Carla De Sola, *Learning Through Dance* (New York: Paulist Press, 1974). The work of Barbara Mettler has also assisted me in helping people to touch into their individual and social experiences through movement and dance. For theory as well as suggested experiences, see Barbara Mettler, *Materials of Dance* (Tucson: Mettler Studios, 1967); idem, *Group Dance Improvisations* (Tucson: Mettler Studios, 1975).

3. For introductions to the benefits of massage, see George Downing, *The Massage Book* (New York: Random House, 1975) and its accompanying meditation book, *Massage and Meditation* (New York: Random House, 1974). See also, Richard Jackson, *Holistic Massage* (New York: Sterling Publishing Company, 1982).

4. See, for example, Ira Progoff, *At a Journal Workshop* (New York: Dialogue House, 1975).

5. For an introduction to the spiritual significance of working with one's dreams, see Robert Schwenck, *Digging Deep* (Pecos, New Mexico: Dove Publications, 1979). For applying the principles of focusing to dream work, see Eugene Gendlin, *Let Your Body Interpret Your Dreams* (Wilmette, Illinois: Chiron Publications, 1986). For a book that captures the playful attitude around dealing with the unconscious as it speaks through dreams, see Robert Bosnak, *A Little Course in Dreams* (Boston: Shambhala Publications, 1988).

Chapter 11

1. Books about the enneagram include the following: Maria Beesing, O.P., Robert J. Nogosek, C.S.C., and Patrick H. O'Leary, S.J., *The Enneagram: A Journey in Self-Discovery* (Denville, New Jersey: Dimension Books, 1984); J. G. Bennett, *Enneagram Studies* (York Beach, Maine: Samuel Weiser, 1983); Margaret Frings Keyes, *Out of the Shadows* (Muir Beach, California: Molysdatur Publications, 1988); Barbara Metz, S.M.D.deN., and John Burchill, O.P., *The Enneagram and Prayer* (Denville, New Jersey: Dimension Books, 1987); P. D. Ouspensky, *In Search of the Miraculous* (New York: Harcourt Brace, 1949); Kathleen Riordan Speeth, in *Transpersonal Psychologies* (New York: Harper and Row, 1975); Jerome P. Wagner, "A Descriptive, Reliability, and Validity Study of the Enneagram Personality Typology," Dissertation Abstracts International (1981), 41, 4664A. This list is not exhaustive, of course.

2. Leonard Cohen, "Joan of Arc," from the album *Famous Blue Raincoat* (Cypress Records; distributed by Poly Gram Records, Inc., New York, 1986). A division of Cypress Entertainment, Inc.; Los Angeles.

3. Thomas Merton, *Bread in the Wilderness* (Collegeville, Minnesota: Liturgical Press, 1953).